Loire Valley Travel Guide 2025

Explore Outdoor Adventures, Natural Heritage, Culture, and Practical Tips

Roberto J. Spivey

All rights reserved. No part of this publication may be reproduced, distributed, or transmitted in any form or by any means, including
photocopying, recording, or other electronic or mechanical methods, without the prior written
permission of the publisher, except in the case of brief quotations embodied in critical reviews and certain other noncommercial uses permitted by copyright law.

Copyright © Roberto J. Spivey, 2024.

To easily explore Loire Valley, simply scan the QR Code with your Smartphone and access interactive Maps.

Table of Contents

Chapter 1: Discovering the Loire Valley 6
- *My Experience in Loire Valley* 8
- *Understanding the UNESCO World Heritage Site* 13
- *Historical Significance Through the Ages* 18
- *Geography and Climate: Best Times to Visit* 22
- *Getting There and Getting Around* 28
- *Essential Travel Planning Tips* 32

Chapter 2: The Royal Route: Châteaux of the Loire 38
- *Chambord: The Crown Jewel* 38
- *Chenonceau: The Ladies' Castle* 43
- *Hidden Gems: Lesser-Known Châteaux* 48
- *Planning Your Castle Route* 53

Chapter 3: Wine Heritage and Gastronomy 58
- *Understanding Loire Valley Wine Regions* 58
- *Premier Vineyards and Wine Routes* 63
- *Wine Tasting Etiquette and Tours* 68
- *Regional Culinary Specialties* 73
- *Farm-to-Table Experiences* 78
- *Michelin-Starred Restaurants and Bistros* 83
- *Food Markets and Local Producers* 88

Chapter 4: Cities and Villages 94
- *Tours: Gateway to the Loire Valley* 94

4

    Orléans: Joan of Arc's City *99*

    Blois: Royal City *103*

    Amboise: Renaissance Glory *109*

    Chinon: Medieval Charm *114*

    Saumur: City of Horses and Wine *119*

    Hidden Villages Worth Discovering *125*

Chapter 5: Outdoor Adventures and Natural Heritage **130**

    Loire à Vélo Cycling Routes *130*

    River Adventures and Loire Marine Life *134*

    Gardens and Parks *138*

    Nature Reserves and Bird Watching *142*

    Walking and Hiking Trails *146*

    Hot Air Balloon Experiences *150*

Chapter 6: Arts, Culture, and Festivals **154**

    Museums and Art Galleries *154*

    Contemporary Art Installations *158*

    Musical Festivals and Performances *162*

    Photography Spots and Tips *166*

Chapter 7: Where to Stay **170**

    Château Hotels *170*

    Boutique Properties *175*

    Historic City Hotels *180*

    Riverside Accommodations *185*

    Rural Gîtes and B&Bs *190*

    Camping and Glamping Options *195*

    Sustainable Stays... *200*

Chapter 8: Practical Information **204**

    Transportation Network... *204*

    Language Tips *208*

    Money Matters... *212*

    Shopping Guide *216*

    Health and Safety... *220*

    Sustainable Tourism Practices.. *224*

    Digital Resources and Apps *228*

Conclusion: Embracing the Loire Valley Spirit **232**

Appendices **236**

    Annual Event Calendar... *236*

    Emergency Contacts and Healthcare Facilities............................... *240*

    Tourist Information Centers *245*

    Useful Phrases in French *249*

Chapter 1: Discovering the Loire Valley

My Experience in Loire Valley

As I stepped off the train at Tours station in the heart of France's Loire Valley, the crisp spring morning air filled my lungs with anticipation. The year was 2024, and I had finally arrived in a region I'd dreamed of visiting since childhood. Little did I know that this journey would become more than just another travel experience – it would transform into a deeply personal adventure that would forever change how I view the world of travel.

The morning sun cast long shadows across the station plaza as I shouldered my backpack, clutching a worn map that would become my constant companion over the next two weeks. My first glimpse of the Loire River stopped me in my tracks. The water sparkled like scattered diamonds, reflecting the early light while hot air balloons dotted the sky above – their vibrant colors creating a striking contrast against the pale blue canvas of morning.

I remember walking along the riverbank that first day, watching local fishermen cast their lines into the gentle waters while sharing animated conversations in rapid French. The smell of fresh-baked croissants wafted from nearby cafés, mixing with the sweet scent of blooming spring flowers. This sensory symphony was just the beginning of what the Loire Valley had in store.

My journey through the valley unfolded like chapters in a beloved book. Each castle told its own story, each vineyard shared its secrets, and every local I met added rich detail to my understanding of this remarkable region. The Château de Chambord emerged from the morning mist like something from a fairy tale, its Renaissance architecture defying belief. I spent hours exploring its 440 rooms, discovering hidden staircases, and imagining the elaborate royal festivities that once filled its halls.

The gardens of Villandry captured my heart in an unexpected way. While other visitors rushed through with their cameras, I found a quiet bench and spent an entire afternoon watching the play of light across the meticulously maintained vegetable gardens. An elderly gardener named Jean-Pierre noticed my interest and shared stories of how his family had tended these gardens for three generations. His weathered hands gestured expressively as he explained the ancient techniques still used to maintain this living work of art.

But the Loire Valley isn't just about grand châteaux and manicured gardens. I discovered this truth in the small village of Montsoreau, where I stumbled upon a weekly market that brought the community to life. Local cheese makers proudly offered samples of their craft, while wine producers shared stories of their families' centuries-old vineyards. An elderly woman named Marie insisted I try her homemade tarte Tatin, a recipe passed down through five generations of her family. The warmth of these encounters taught me that the true magic of the Loire Valley lives in its people.

The wine caves of Vouvray revealed another dimension of the region's character. Deep underground, where the temperature remains constant year-round, I learned about the patient art of wine making from passionate vintners who spoke about their craft with reverence. The cool, damp air and centuries-old tunnels created an atmosphere that transported me back in time, making me feel connected to the countless generations who had worked in these same caves.

My most memorable evening was spent in a small family-run vineyard near Chinon. The owner, Philippe, invited me to join his family for dinner after a wine tasting session ran late. We sat in their ancient kitchen, where wooden beams crossed the ceiling and a massive fireplace dominated one wall. Over a simple but exquisite meal of local specialties, they shared stories that spanned generations. Their teenage daughter practiced her English with me, while their grandmother insisted on teaching me traditional Loire Valley folk songs.

As I explored more of the region, I began to understand that the Loire Valley isn't just a destination – it's a living, breathing entity that changes with the seasons. I watched spring flowers bloom in castle gardens, tasted wines that captured the essence of the terrain, and discovered hidden paths that led to unexpected treasures. Each day brought new discoveries: a forgotten chapel covered in ancient frescoes, a riverside picnic spot known only to locals, or a family restaurant serving recipes unchanged for centuries.

This guide grew from my experiences, my encounters, and my discoveries. It's more than just a collection of recommendations – it's a companion for your own journey through this enchanting region. In the chapters that follow, I'll share detailed insights about the places that captured my heart, and the experiences that made my journey unforgettable.

You'll learn about hidden gems that most tourists never see, discover the best times to visit popular sites to avoid crowds, and find out how to connect with local communities in meaningful ways.

Understanding the UNESCO World Heritage Site

Standing at the majestic Château d'Amboise in 2024, gazing across the sweeping Loire River valley, I found myself transported back to the moment in 2000 when UNESCO recognized this magnificent landscape as a World Heritage Site. The morning sun illuminated the limestone facades of the château, while vineyards stretched toward the horizon like a living masterpiece – a scene that has captivated visitors for centuries.

The Loire Valley's UNESCO designation spans an impressive 280 kilometers, flowing from Sully-sur-Loire to Chalonnes-sur-Loire. This protected area embraces not just the mighty river itself, but extends across both banks to encompass historic towns, architectural treasures, and agricultural lands that have shaped human civilization for over two millennia.

Walking through the streets of Blois, I spoke with Marie-Claire, a local heritage conservator who has dedicated her life to preserving this remarkable region. She shared how the UNESCO recognition emerged from the valley's exceptional demonstration of human creativity and innovation. The area secured its prestigious status by meeting multiple UNESCO criteria, highlighting both its cultural significance and the harmonious relationship between people and nature.

The architectural heritage of the Loire Valley stands as a testament to centuries of human ingenuity. Renaissance châteaux rise from medieval foundations, while Romanesque churches nestle within ancient villages. In Chambord, I watched restoration experts meticulously repair intricate stonework using traditional techniques passed down through generations. Their dedication ensures these architectural marvels will inspire future visitors just as they amazed me.

The cultural landscape stretches beyond individual monuments. Traditional wine-making practices continue in centuries-old caves carved into limestone cliffs. In Vouvray, I met Pierre, a fifth-generation vintner who explained how UNESCO status helps preserve not just the physical vineyards, but the ancient knowledge and customs that make Loire Valley wines unique. His eyes sparkled with pride as he described how sustainable farming practices protect both the terroir and local biodiversity.

The Loire Valley's inscription recognizes the extraordinary way humans have shaped – and been shaped by – this river landscape over two thousand years. Roman bridges still stand alongside medieval market towns, while Renaissance gardens blend seamlessly into working farmland. This living heritage continues to evolve while maintaining its historical integrity.

Conservation efforts have intensified since the UNESCO designation. Local authorities collaborate with international experts to protect both natural and cultural assets. In Chenonceau, I observed how careful water management preserves the château's famous gallery spanning the Cher River while supporting local ecosystem health. Modern technology now monitors structural stability without compromising historical authenticity.

The management plan for this vast heritage site requires delicate balance. Communities must develop economically while preserving their cultural identity. In Amboise, local officials explained how they regulate new construction to maintain historical viewscapes while meeting contemporary needs. Traditional craftspeople receive support to continue their work, ensuring ancient skills survive in a modern economy.

Tourism policies have evolved significantly under UNESCO guidelines. Visitor management strategies now protect sensitive sites from overcrowding while enhancing guest experiences. Small group tours led by local experts have replaced mass tourism at many locations. These changes allow more meaningful connections between visitors and this extraordinary landscape.

The World Heritage status has transformed how local communities view their heritage. In Saumur, I attended a town meeting where residents debated future development plans. Their passionate discussions revealed deep commitment to preserving their cultural legacy while building a sustainable future. Young people spoke about innovative ways to adapt historical buildings for modern uses while respecting their original character.

Research programs supported by UNESCO status continue to uncover new aspects of Loire Valley heritage. Archaeologists working near Tours recently discovered previously unknown medieval wine cellars, adding another layer to our understanding of the region's viticultural history. Each finding helps refine conservation strategies and enriches visitor experiences.

The Loire Valley's protected status has sparked renewed interest in traditional crafts and customs. Local schools now include heritage education in their curricula, ensuring young generations understand and value their cultural inheritance. Apprenticeship programs pair experienced artisans with students eager to learn historical building techniques and traditional arts.

Climate change presents new challenges for heritage preservation. Conservation teams are developing innovative strategies to protect vulnerable sites from increasing flood risks and temperature fluctuations. These efforts demonstrate how UNESCO status helps mobilize resources and expertise to address emerging threats to cultural heritage.

Historical Significance Through the Ages

The Loire Valley tells a story spanning 40,000 years, beginning when prehistoric hunters carved shelters into its soft tufa cliffs. Standing in these ancient caves near Saumur today, touching the cool limestone walls, visitors can sense the profound connection to those first human inhabitants who recognized the valley's life-sustaining potential.

Celtic tribes established the first permanent settlements around 800 BCE, leaving behind mysterious stone monuments and burial mounds. Their sacred sites, particularly near Amboise, demonstrate sophisticated astronomical knowledge. Modern archaeologists continue uncovering

Celtic artifacts that reveal a complex society thriving along the river's fertile banks.

When Roman legions arrived in 52 BCE, they transformed the valley into a vital commercial artery. They constructed the first bridges spanning the Loire, engineered roads that still influence modern pathways, and founded cities including Tours and Orléans. Roman architectural innovations persist in surviving aqueducts and amphitheaters, while excavated villa foundations near Chinon reveal elaborate mosaic floors depicting river commerce.

The medieval period dawned with dramatic changes following Rome's retreat. Local nobles constructed wooden fortresses atop strategic hilltops, gradually replacing them with stone castles. The feudal system emerged, centered around these fortified strongholds. Visiting Langeais Castle today, built in 992 CE, provides vivid insights into medieval military architecture and daily life.

The 11th century marked a spiritual awakening, when magnificent Romanesque abbeys arose along pilgrimage routes. The Abbey of Fleury at Saint-Benoît-sur-Loire stands testament to this era, its tower reaching skyward while intricate carved capitals tell biblical stories through stone. Monks cultivated vineyards, establishing viticultural traditions that continue shaping the region.

The Hundred Years' War (1337-1453) brought Joan of Arc to prominence in the Loire Valley. Her miraculous victory at Orléans in 1429 turned the tide against English forces. The fortress where she met with Charles VII still dominates Chinon's skyline, allowing visitors to walk the very halls where history shifted course.

The Renaissance transformed the Loire Valley into France's royal heartland. When François I assumed the throne in 1515, he initiated an architectural revolution. The king invited Italian artists and architects to reimagine medieval fortresses into pleasure palaces. Leonardo da Vinci arrived at Amboise in 1516, bringing revolutionary artistic and engineering ideas that influenced château design throughout the region.
Château de Chambord, François I's crowning achievement begun in 1519, exemplifies Renaissance innovation. Its double-helix staircase, reportedly designed by Leonardo, demonstrates the period's mathematical and architectural brilliance. Each of the 440 rooms showcases Renaissance ideals of symmetry and grandeur.

Catherine de' Medici's influence peaked during the 1550s and 1560s, when she commissioned extensive gardens at Chenonceau. Her sophisticated Italianate designs revolutionized French landscape architecture. Today's visitors can still stroll paths she envisioned, experiencing how Renaissance concepts of formal garden design harmonized nature with human aesthetic desires.

The Loire Valley's golden age extended through the 16th century as successive monarchs expanded their architectural legacy. Henri II and Diane de Poitiers transformed Chenonceau into its current form, spanning the River Cher with an elegant gallery that served both practical and aesthetic purposes. This architectural feat remains unique in world architecture.

The region's significance shifted during the 17th century when Louis XIV centralized power at Versailles. Yet this departure preserved the Loire Valley's Renaissance character, freezing it in time. While other regions modernized, the Loire's châteaux maintained their 16th-century splendor, creating living museum of Renaissance architecture and culture that draws millions annually.

Geography and Climate: Best Times to Visit

The Loire River meanders through central France like a liquid ribbon, carving a gentle valley that stretches 1,012 kilometers from its source in the Massif Central to the Atlantic Ocean. This majestic waterway shapes both the physical landscape and the daily rhythms of life in the valley, creating distinct microclimates that have blessed the region with agricultural abundance for millennia.

The river system includes major tributaries – the Cher, Indre, and Vienne – which join the main channel at strategic points, creating fertile floodplains and dramatic limestone cliffs. These geological features emerged over millions of years, leaving behind the tuffeau stone that medieval builders would later use to construct the region's iconic châteaux.

Maritime influences from the Atlantic moderate the valley's climate, pushing warm, moist air inland throughout the year. This creates milder winters than surrounding regions, while summer temperatures remain pleasantly warm without reaching extremes. The interplay between ocean breezes and continental air masses generates the perfect conditions for wine cultivation, especially in protected slopes facing south and southeast.

January brings crisp mornings with average temperatures between 3°C and 8°C. Winter mists roll off the river, shrouding châteaux in mysterious veils until mid-morning. While rainfall averages 63mm, winter visitors enjoy peaceful exploration of historical sites without summer crowds. The bare trees reveal architectural details usually hidden by foliage, making this season ideal for photography enthusiasts.

Spring arrives gradually through March and April, with temperatures climbing to 12-18°C. Cherry blossoms burst forth in château gardens, while early wildflowers carpet woodland floors. April showers (averaging 58mm) alternate with sunny spells, creating dramatic skies perfect for photography. Morning balloon flights resume during this period, offering breathtaking views of the awakening landscape.

May emerges with temperatures between 15-22°C and declining rainfall (56mm). Gardens reach peak bloom, making this month ideal for visiting Villandry and Chenonceau. Cycling becomes particularly pleasant along riverside paths, with warm afternoons and cool mornings providing perfect conditions for outdoor activities.

Summer sunshine bathes the valley from June through August, with temperatures ranging from 18-28°C. Long daylight hours (up to 16 hours) allow extended exploration of outdoor sites. July and August bring the warmest weather, though afternoon temperatures rarely exceed 30°C thanks to river breezes. Morning hours offer the most comfortable conditions for château visits, while evenings prove perfect for wine tasting in cool cave cellars.

September heralds harvest season, with temperatures moderating to 15-23°C. Morning mists create magical conditions for photography, while stable weather patterns make this month ideal for outdoor activities. Wine enthusiasts particularly prize this period for visiting vineyards during vendange (grape harvest).

October paints the valley in autumn colors, with temperatures ranging from 11-18°C. Rainfall increases slightly (64mm), but between showers, clear skies and fall foliage create spectacular backdrops for château photography. The tourist crowds thin considerably, allowing more intimate exploration of historical sites.

November and December return the valley to winter quiet. Temperatures drop to 5-12°C, while rainfall reaches annual peaks (69mm in November). However, château interiors maintain constant temperatures year-round, making these months excellent for exploring historical collections and architecture.

Climate change impacts have become increasingly apparent since 2020. Earlier spring blooming affects garden displays, while summer heat waves occur more frequently. Winter flooding events have intensified, occasionally affecting river-level attractions. Visitors planning future trips should consider these shifts, particularly when timing garden visits or river activities.

Seasonal weather patterns profoundly influence visitor experiences throughout the Loire Valley, with each month offering unique opportunities and challenges. Early spring mornings might greet cyclists with ground fog rising from the river, creating ethereal scenes around château towers, yet by mid-morning, bright sunshine often burns through the mist, revealing vivid garden colors against blue skies.

The valley's elevation variations, though subtle, play crucial roles in local weather conditions. The gentle slopes of vineyard sites, typically ranging from 30 to 150 meters above sea level, create natural drainage patterns that protect vines from frost damage. Local vignerons have learned to read these topographical nuances, planting different grape varieties according to elevation and sun exposure.

Loire Valley soil composition varies remarkably within short distances. The famous tuffeau limestone dominates central regions, while sandy soils prevail near river confluences. This geological diversity creates distinctive terroirs, affecting not just wine production but also garden designs and architectural choices throughout history.

Regional microclimates demonstrate fascinating variations. The Touraine area experiences slightly warmer temperatures than surrounding regions due to urban heat effects around Tours, while the Anjou sector receives more rainfall owing to Atlantic influences. Understanding these patterns helps travelers plan castle visits and outdoor activities effectively.
Wind patterns shift seasonally, with prevailing westerlies bringing Atlantic moisture during winter months. Summer often sees gentler breezes, making morning balloon flights particularly stable from June through September. Local operators track wind patterns meticulously, scheduling flights when conditions promise optimal visibility and comfort.

Humidity levels fluctuate significantly throughout the year, averaging 75-85% during winter mornings but dropping to

45-60% on summer afternoons. This variation affects both comfort levels and photographic conditions, particularly during early morning château visits when mist often creates dramatic scenes around river-spanning structures like Chenonceau.

Spring frost remains a concern through early May, particularly affecting garden displays and vineyard production. Historic châteaux have developed traditional methods to protect their formal gardens, including temporary greenhouses and strategic planting schedules. Modern climate change has made these frost patterns less predictable, requiring more flexible visiting strategies.

Summer thunderstorms typically develop during late afternoons, especially in July and August. These brief but intense weather events create opportunities for dramatic photography but can interrupt outdoor activities. Experienced travelers learn to schedule morning visits to exposed sites, reserving indoor activities for potentially stormy afternoon hours.

The Loire Valley's position, roughly halfway between the equator and North Pole, provides balanced daylight hours that benefit travelers. Summer days stretch gloriously long, with first light appearing around 5:30 AM and dusk lingering past 10:00 PM. Winter brings shorter but still manageable days, with approximately eight hours of usable daylight for exploration.

Getting There and Getting Around

International Access Points

The Loire Valley beckons travelers through several convenient gateways. Paris Charles de Gaulle Airport serves major international carriers, placing visitors just two hours from the heart of château country. Nantes Atlantique Airport, nestled near the valley's western edge, welcomes European flights and connects seamlessly to regional transport networks. The smaller Tours Val de Loire Airport handles domestic French routes, landing travelers directly in the valley's center.

High-Speed Rail Networks

The TGV high-speed rail system transforms the journey into part of the adventure. Sleek trains glide from Paris Montparnasse station to Tours in a mere 75 minutes, racing through picturesque countryside at speeds reaching 320 kilometers per hour. Multiple daily departures between 6:00 AM and 10:00 PM provide flexibility, while first-class carriages offer panoramic windows perfect for soaking in initial glimpses of the landscape.

Booking strategies matter significantly with TGV travel. Purchasing tickets three months ahead through SNCF's website or app typically secures fares 40-60% below last-minute prices. Senior travelers should investigate the "Carte Senior+" rail discount card, which pays itself back within two round trips from Paris.

Regional Transportation Network

The regional TER train system weaves together Loire Valley communities like pearls on a string. Regular services connect Tours, Blois, Amboise, and Orléans, with tickets costing substantially less than TGV fares. These trains stop at smaller stations near major châteaux, simplifying day trips without rental car hassles.

Regional buses complement train services, reaching locations beyond rail lines. The Rémi network offers comprehensive coverage with modern, air-conditioned coaches. Multi-day passes provide excellent value, while real-time tracking apps help plan connections precisely.

Driving in the Loire Valley

Rental car agencies cluster around major train stations, offering freedom to explore remote villages and hidden vineyards. International driving permits prove essential, obtainable from automobile associations before departure. Most châteaux provide ample parking, though summer visits might require early arrival at popular sites like Chambord.

French driving customs deserve attention. Speed cameras monitor major routes vigilantly, while roundabouts follow strict right-of-way protocols. Rural roads meander through villages where priority rules differ from highways. Fuel stations become scarce in countryside areas - maintaining at least half tank ensures peaceful exploration.

Loire à Vélo Cycling Network

The Loire à Vélo route spans 900 kilometers of dedicated cycling paths, transforming the valley into a cyclist's paradise. Well-maintained trails follow riverbanks and cross vineyards, connecting major sites while avoiding vehicular traffic. Clear signage indicates distances, difficulty levels, and nearby amenities.

Bike rental operations in every major town offer various options, from basic city bikes to premium electric models. Advance reservations become crucial during peak season (June-September). Many operators provide luggage transfer services, allowing multi-day rides between accommodations without heavy bags.

Essential Travel Planning Tips

Planning Loire Valley adventures begins months before departure. Passports must remain valid six months beyond intended stay dates while France's Schengen visa requirements vary by nationality. Travel insurance becomes crucial, particularly when booking château tours or wine experiences with strict cancellation policies. Reservations during peak season (June-September) demand booking three to four months ahead, especially luxury accommodations within historic properties.

Banking and Currency Matters

The Loire Valley's financial landscape blends modern convenience with rural traditions. While château gift shops and established restaurants accept major credit cards, smaller family vineyards and local markets often prefer cash transactions. French banks typically charge lower ATM fees than currency exchange offices, though withdrawing larger amounts less frequently minimizes transaction costs.

Smart travelers notify their banks about French travel dates, preventing automated fraud detection systems from blocking cards. Carrying a modest emergency cash reserve proves wise, particularly when exploring remote villages where ATMs might be scarce. Local banks generally open 9:00 AM-

5:00 PM Tuesday through Saturday, closing Monday mornings and Sunday entirely.

Seasonal Packing Strategies

Spring travelers need layered clothing combinations. Light raincoats protect against sudden showers while removable layers accommodate temperature variations between sunny afternoons and cool castle interiors. Comfortable walking shoes with good grip handle both cobblestone streets and château gardens.

Summer demands lightweight, breathable fabrics and sun protection. Wide-brimmed hats shield faces during garden tours while refillable water bottles become essential during cycling adventures. Evening temperatures can drop significantly, requiring light sweaters or jackets for outdoor dining.

Autumn brings variable conditions requiring versatile wardrobes. Water-resistant boots protect feet during vineyard visits, while scarves and gloves prove valuable during early morning château photography sessions. Multiple thin layers offer more flexibility than single thick garments.

Winter visitors need warm, waterproof clothing. Thermal underlayers maintain comfort during outdoor activities while weatherproof outerwear resists cold winds along the Loire

River. Sturdy boots with non-slip soles safely navigate potentially icy palace steps.

Technology Considerations

Mobile connectivity shapes modern Loire Valley exploration. Local SIM cards provide cheaper data rates than international roaming, available from carriers in larger towns. Public Wi-Fi networks exist in tourist areas, though connection speeds vary considerably.

Essential apps include rail booking platforms, wine route maps, and château visit planners. Offline navigation capabilities prove invaluable in rural areas with limited mobile coverage. External battery packs extend device life during full-day excursions.

French power outlets require type C or E adapters delivering 230V current. Quality surge protectors safeguard sensitive electronics, while dual-voltage chargers eliminate transformer needs. Many historic hotels offer limited electrical outlets, making multiple-port USB chargers practical.

Cultural Awareness

French social customs emphasize politeness and respect. Basic French phrases demonstrate cultural appreciation - simple greetings like "Bonjour" (hello) and "Merci" (thank you) open doors to warmer interactions. Restaurant

34

reservations follow strict timing, with lunch typically served 12:00-2:00 PM and dinner 7:00-10:00 PM.

Accessibility Planning

Historic sites increasingly prioritize accessibility. Many châteaux have installed elevators and ramps, though limited modifications preserve architectural authenticity. Specialized tour operators arrange accessible transportation between sites, while hotels offer adapted rooms when booked well ahead. Mobility equipment rentals deliver directly to accommodations, ensuring comfort throughout the stay.

Sustainable Tourism

The Loire Valley's delicate ecosystem deserves protection through mindful travel choices. Reusable water bottles refill safely from public fountains while locally produced bags suit shopping needs. Choosing locally owned accommodations, restaurants, and guides strengthens community connections while reducing environmental impact. Bicycle tours and walking paths offer low-impact exploration alternatives to driving.

Visiting wine producers who practice sustainable viticulture supports traditional agricultural methods. Many family-owned vineyards maintain centuries-old practices that protect soil health and biodiversity. Selecting these producers encourages preservation of both environmental and cultural heritage.

Morning visits to popular sites reduce afternoon air conditioning needs in historic buildings. Supporting local markets and craft producers minimizes transportation impact while preserving traditional skills. Small group tours optimize resource use while providing more intimate experiences with local culture.

Health and Safety

Medical preparation ensures peace of mind. European Health Insurance Cards benefit EU residents, while other travelers need comprehensive coverage. Local pharmacies, marked by green crosses, stock common medications and offer professional advice in multiple languages. Emergency services respond quickly throughout the region, with major hospitals located in larger towns.

Loire Valley adventures blend careful planning with spontaneous discovery. Each preparation detail enhances the journey, creating space for magical moments among historic châteaux and timeless villages. The effort invested in thoughtful planning transforms simple visits into profound connections with this extraordinary landscape.

Through informed preparation and respectful travel practices, modern adventurers participate in preserving the Loire Valley's remarkable heritage. These conscientious choices ensure future generations will discover their own enchanting moments in this magnificent region, carrying forward centuries of cultural tradition and natural beauty.

This careful balance between thorough planning and openness to serendipity creates the foundation for truly memorable Loire Valley experiences. Every considered detail contributes to deeper appreciation of this remarkable destination, where history, culture, and natural beauty intertwine in endless fascinating ways.

Chapter 2: The Royal Route: Châteaux of the Loire

Chambord: The Crown Jewel

Rising majestically from the misty forests of Sologne, Château de Chambord stands testament to the boundless ambition of François I. Located at 41250 Chambord, France, this architectural marvel beckons visitors into a world where French Renaissance dreams materialized in stone. The château's scale remains breathtaking - 440 rooms, 282 fireplaces, and 84 staircases spread across 156 meters of façade.

The year 1519 marked the beginning of this extraordinary venture. François I, fresh from his encounters with Italian Renaissance genius, envisioned more than mere hunting lodge. His ambition called forth master masons, sculptors, and possibly Leonardo da Vinci himself to create something unprecedented in architectural history.

The double-helix staircase forms Chambord's beating heart. Two independent spiral staircases intertwine around a central column, never meeting yet ascending four stories in perfect mathematical harmony. This revolutionary design bears Leonardo's unmistakable influence - each staircase allows continuous movement, with people ascending never crossing paths with those descending. Standing at its base, looking upward through the spiraling void creates an almost hypnotic effect, drawing eyes toward the intricate vaulted ceiling above.

Chambord's roofscape tells stories through stone. Eleven types of towers and three types of chimneys create what appears chaotic at first glance but reveals precise mathematical order upon closer inspection. These elevated architectural elements represent a medieval French castle turned inside out - defensive features transformed into decorative statements. Each tower, chimney, and lantern holds symbolic significance, from royal salamanders to intertwined initials marking François I's legacy.

Visiting hours shift seasonally: 9:00 AM to 5:00 PM from October through March, extending to 6:00 PM April through September. Early morning arrival, particularly before 10:00 AM, rewards visitors with sublime light conditions and smaller crowds. The first sunbeams striking the limestone façade create otherworldly photography opportunities, especially from the northwestern approach.

Ticket prices reflect experience levels: basic entry (14.50€), guided tours (22€), and premium experiences including tower access (35€). Annual passes prove economical for multiple visits, while combination tickets with nearby châteaux offer significant savings.

Photography enthusiasts should note several prime vantage points. The formal gardens, restored to their 18th-century glory, provide classical façade views. The lesser-known northeastern corner offers compelling angles of the chapel tower against morning light. Inside, natural light streaming through lancet windows creates dramatic effects on the spiral staircase between 11:00 AM and 2:00 PM.

Hidden architectural details reward patient observers. Carved salamanders, François I's emblem, appear in unexpected places throughout the château. The second-floor ceiling in the northeast tower bears mason's marks rarely noticed by visitors. The king's private chapel contains subtle astronomical alignments visible only during equinoxes.

The restored French formal gardens provide context often missed in historic illustrations. These gardens, recreated using 18th-century plans, demonstrate how the château originally integrated with its landscape. Winter visits reveal the geometric precision of their design, while summer showcases lavender beds and precisely trimmed topiary.

Seasonal events transform the visitor experience. Summer evening sound-and-light shows project historical scenes onto the façade, while December brings period-appropriate Christmas decorations. Special exhibitions rotate through the royal apartments, often highlighting lesser-known aspects of château history.

The surrounding 13,000-acre forest, France's largest walled woodland, preserves the château's original hunting-lodge context. Walking trails allow visitors to experience approaches similar to those used by 16th-century guests. Dawn and dusk often reveal deer and wild boar, maintaining living connections to the château's sporting heritage.

Chambord ultimately transcends mere architecture - it embodies Renaissance ideals of harmony between human ambition and mathematical precision. Each visit reveals new details, new perspectives, and deeper appreciation for this magnificent achievement in stone. The château continues inspiring visitors just as it inspired its creators five centuries ago, standing proud against the sky as France's ultimate expression of Renaissance vision.

Chenonceau: The Ladies' Castle

Located at 37150 Chenonceaux, France, Château de Chenonceau graces the Cher River like a vision from a fairy tale, its elegant architecture reflecting perfectly in the water below. This remarkable palace, often called the "Ladies' Castle," tells the story of remarkable women who shaped both its architecture and its destiny across five centuries.

Katherine Briçonnet initiated Chenonceau's transformation in 1513, overseeing construction while her husband served the French crown. Her architectural vision established the château's distinctive style, combining Gothic tradition with Renaissance innovation. The original medieval fortress disappeared beneath her refined design, though remnants remain visible in the chapel's foundations.

Diane de Poitiers, beloved of Henri II, received Chenonceau in 1547. Her sophisticated taste transformed the grounds, creating magnificent gardens along the river's northern bank. These formal plantings, recently restored to their 16th-century glory, showcase geometric patterns best viewed from the château's upper windows. Diane also commissioned the remarkable bridge spanning the Cher River, engineering feat that would later inspire the château's most famous feature.

Catherine de Medici claimed Chenonceau upon Henri II's death in 1559, compelling Diane to exchange it for Chaumont. Catherine's lasting contribution, the two-story gallery atop Diane's bridge, created the château's iconic silhouette. This magnificent space, stretching 60 meters across the river, hosted France's first fireworks display during a spectacular party in 1560. Today, visitors walking these rooms sense echoes of Renaissance court life through preserved period furnishings and royal portraits.

The gallery served crucial roles during both World Wars. From 1914-1918, it functioned as a military hospital, its river-spanning position allowing wounded soldiers to arrive directly by boat. During World War II, the gallery provided an escape route between Nazi-occupied France and the free zone - the Cher River marked the boundary. The château's wartime history comes alive through photographs and documents displayed in the former servants' quarters.

Visiting Chenonceau demands strategic timing. Opening hours span 9:30 AM to 5:30 PM in winter (mid-November through February) and extend to 7:00 PM during peak season (March through mid-November). Early morning visits, particularly before 10:00 AM, offer optimal photography conditions and smaller crowds. The afternoon sun creates stunning reflections on the river between 2:00 PM and 4:00 PM.

The wine cellars, housed in the original 16th-century foundations, invite exploration through guided tours (included with admission). These atmospheric spaces showcase regional wines, with tastings available during afternoon sessions. The adjacent flower workshop demonstrates the château's continuing tradition of fresh floral arrangements - every room receives new compositions weekly, requiring thousands of blooms grown in on-site gardens.

Seasonal events transform the visitor experience. Summer evening illuminations cast magical reflections across the river, while Christmas brings period decorations and special concerts in the gallery. Spring showcases tulip displays in

Diane's garden, while autumn paints surrounding forests in spectacular colors.

Photography enthusiasts discover multiple prime vantage points. The small bridge downstream offers classic views of the château reflected in still morning waters. The Renaissance garden provides elevated perspectives of the architecture, while the wooded park reveals unexpected angles through seasonal foliage. Early evening light bathes the western façade in golden hues perfect for capturing architectural details.

The château's interior reveals intimate glimpses of its famous residents. Catherine de Medici's study contains original 16th-century flooring and ceiling beams. The bedchambers showcase period furnishings, while the kitchens maintain their original copper cookware. Each room tells stories through carefully preserved artifacts and artistic treasures.

Chenonceau stands testament to the power of feminine vision in French history. From Katherine's architectural innovation through Catherine's political genius, these remarkable women created more than mere palace - they shaped a living masterpiece that continues inspiring visitors today. Every aspect, from the meticulously maintained gardens to the historic art collections, reflects their enduring influence on French culture and architecture.

This extraordinary château rewards thoughtful exploration at any season, offering fresh perspectives with each visit. Whether illuminated by morning mist or evening sun, Chenonceau maintains its reputation as the Loire Valley's most romantic and historically significant château.

Hidden Gems: Lesser-Known Châteaux

Château de Villandry stands at 3 Rue Principale, 37510 Villandry, France, celebrating the perfect marriage between architecture and horticulture. While other Loire châteaux overwhelm with their grandeur, Villandry captivates through mathematical precision expressed in living plants. The Renaissance château presents classical proportions, but the true magic unfolds in its surroundings - six distinct gardens spread across three terraces, each telling its own story through meticulously maintained plantings.

The decorative vegetable garden, perhaps Europe's largest, transforms practical agriculture into living art. Nine identical squares showcase geometric patterns created from cabbage, carrots, leeks, and other edibles, their colors and textures changing with each season. The love garden expresses romantic themes through carefully trimmed boxwood, while the water garden provides serene reflection pools perfect for early morning photography.

Visiting hours run 9:00 AM to 5:00 PM (November-March) and 9:00 AM to 7:00 PM (April-October). Early morning visits allow photographers to capture mist rising from the gardens, while late afternoon light creates dramatic shadows across the geometric patterns. The château interior reveals

Renaissance architectural details, but the gardens demand most attention, particularly during spring planting and fall harvest.

Château d'Ussé rises like a fairy tale vision at 37420 Rigny-Ussé, France. This stunning white limestone castle allegedly inspired Charles Perrault's "Sleeping Beauty," and walking its ramparts easily sparks imagination. The medieval fortress core gradually transformed into an elegant Renaissance residence, while 17th-century additions created the romantic silhouette visible today.

The château's unique features include fully furnished period rooms bringing past centuries alive. The kitchen maintains its original copper cookware, while the guard room displays impressive arms and armor collections. The tower rooms house a charming "Sleeping Beauty" exhibition, complete with period-costumed mannequins illustrating the famous tale.

Operating hours span 10:00 AM to 6:00 PM (April-September) and 10:00 AM to 5:00 PM (October-March). Morning visits avoid tour bus crowds, while late afternoon light bathes the white towers in golden hues perfect for photography. The surrounding park provides excellent vantage points for capturing the château's fairy tale appearance.

Château de Chinon commands attention from its rocky promontory at Rue du Château, 37500 Chinon, France. This impressive fortress witnessed pivotal moments in French history, most notably Joan of Arc's first meeting with Charles VII in 1429. The massive complex spreads across three distinct sections, each revealing different architectural periods and defensive innovations.

The royal quarters preserve medieval domestic architecture, while the impressive keep demonstrates military engineering excellence. Recent restorations have added glass-floored walkways allowing visitors to examine archaeological discoveries beneath their feet. The Clock Tower houses an impressive museum detailing the fortress's role in French history.

Visiting hours extend from 9:30 AM to 5:00 PM (October-March) and 9:30 AM to 7:00 PM (April-September). Morning fog often shrouds the fortress dramatically, while afternoon sun highlights the imposing stonework. The ramparts provide spectacular views across the Vienne River valley and surrounding vineyards.

These less-visited châteaux reward thoughtful exploration. Combining visits requires strategic planning - Villandry and Ussé pair naturally, while Chinon demands dedicated time due to its size and historical significance. Local restaurants near each château offer authentic regional cuisine, providing perfect midday breaks between visits.

Each castle tells unique stories through architecture and landscape. Villandry demonstrates Renaissance ideals of harmony between human design and natural beauty. Ussé captures imagination through romantic architecture and literary connections. Chinon reveals medieval military power while preserving pivotal moments in French history.

These hidden gems provide more intimate experiences than their famous neighbors. Smaller crowds allow deeper appreciation of architectural details and historical significance. Whether photographing Villandry's geometric gardens at dawn, exploring Ussé's fairy tale towers, or walking Chinon's historic ramparts, each visit creates lasting connections to Loire Valley heritage.

Planning Your Castle Route

The Loire Valley châteaux weave together like chapters in an epic historical novel. Thoughtful route planning transforms individual visits into cohesive narratives, revealing connections between architecture, history, and landscape. Strategic itineraries maximize limited time while minimizing travel fatigue.

Two-Day Essential Experience

Base yourself in Tours or Amboise, each offering excellent train connections and accommodation options. Begin early at Chambord, arriving when morning mist still wreaths its spectacular roofline. Spend the morning exploring this architectural masterpiece, then travel to Chenonceau after lunch. The afternoon light creates perfect reflections of Chenonceau in the Cher River, while evening crowds thin considerably after 4:00 PM.

Day two focuses on Amboise and Clos Lucé, connected by Leonardo da Vinci's legacy. Morning hours suit Amboise's elevated position, offering spectacular views across the Loire. Afternoon at Clos Lucé reveals Leonardo's workshops and inventions, completing this Renaissance-themed journey.

Five-Day Royal History Route

53

Establish base in Blois, perfectly positioned between major sites. Start with Blois château itself, whose four distinct wings introduce major architectural periods. Afternoon visits to nearby Cheverny showcase later architectural evolution and hunting traditions.

Days two and three mirror the two-day itinerary but with relaxed pacing allowing deeper exploration. The extra time permits garden visits at Chenonceau and rooftop tours at Chambord. Evening sound-and-light shows at both châteaux become possible with this schedule.

Days four and five venture westward to Villandry and Azay-le-Rideau. Villandry's gardens demand morning visits when light angles showcase their geometric patterns. Azay-le-Rideau's romantic moat setting proves most photogenic during late afternoon.

Week-Long Comprehensive Journey

Extended stays allow exploration beyond major sites. Base-hopping between Blois, Tours, and Saumur provides access to different château clusters while minimizing daily travel time.

Begin in Blois following the five-day schedule, then shift focus toward lesser-known gems. Chaumont's garden festival deserves full-day appreciation. Ussé's fairy tale atmosphere and Chinon's medieval power complement each other perfectly when paired.

Later days might include Langeais, whose furnished interiors best preserve medieval domestic life, or Loches, whose massive keep demonstrates military architecture's evolution. Final days in Saumur allow wine cave exploration between château visits.

Thematic Routes

Medieval Military Architecture:
- Start at Chinon's impressive fortifications
- Continue to Loches' massive keep
- Finish at Langeais' transition architecture
- Perfect during cloudy days when photography proves challenging

Renaissance Innovation:
- Begin with Chambord's revolutionary design
- Move to Leonardo's work at Clos Lucé
- End at Amboise, connecting both sites
- Best appreciated during shoulder seasons when crowds thin

Garden Enthusiasts:
- Morning at Villandry's geometric masterpiece

- Afternoon comparing Chenonceau's distinct garden styles
- Next day at Chaumont's contemporary garden festival
- Schedule during peak blooming seasons (May-September)

Seasonal Considerations

Spring offers optimal garden viewing and moderate crowds. Summer crowds demand early arrival strategies but allow evening events. Autumn provides spectacular color backgrounds and harvest activities. Winter reveals architectural details normally hidden by foliage.

Photography Tips

Dawn mist creates ethereal château settings, particularly at river-side locations. Mid-morning light suits elevated sites like Amboise. Afternoon sun enhances garden photography at Villandry and Chenonceau. Dusk illumination transforms château facades during sound-and-light seasons.

These routes adapt easily to weather conditions. Rainy days suit interior-focused visits to furnished châteaux like Cheverny, while clear weather favors garden-heavy itineraries. The dense château network allows flexible rescheduling without losing valuable exploration time.

Careful planning transforms Loire Valley exploration into seamless historical narratives. Whether following royal footsteps through centuries of architectural innovation or tracing garden design evolution across multiple sites, thoughtful itineraries enhance understanding while preventing château fatigue. Each visit builds upon previous experiences, creating rich, multi-layered appreciation of this remarkable heritage landscape.

Chapter 3: Wine Heritage and Gastronomy

Understanding Loire Valley Wine Regions

The Loire Valley's viticultural tapestry stretches like a sinuous ribbon along France's longest river, weaving through landscapes that have nurtured wine cultivation since Roman times. Standing amidst these vineyards in 2024, watching morning mist rise from the Loire River, reveals why this region earned its "Garden of France" moniker.

The valley's unique geography creates a perfect storm of conditions for exceptional winemaking. The Loire River moderates temperatures while channeling cool Atlantic influences inland, protecting vines from spring frosts and scorching summers. This climate dance produces wines with bright acidity and lower alcohol content, hallmarks that have gained renewed appreciation in recent years as wine enthusiasts seek elegance over power.

Each wine region tells its distinct story through soil and grape. Beginning near the Atlantic, Pays Nantais presents granite and metamorphic rock soils where Melon de Bourgogne grapes transform into crisp Muscadet wines. These wines carry whispers of sea spray and minerals, reflecting their maritime heritage. Local vignerons have revolutionized Muscadet production through extended lees aging, creating wines with remarkable complexity and aging potential.

Moving inland, Anjou-Saumur's landscape shifts dramatically. Here, limestone caves carved into tuffeau rock provide perfect aging conditions. This chalky bedrock, combined with sections of schist and slate, nurtures Chenin Blanc vines that produce both bone-dry and luxuriously sweet wines. The fascinating contrast between Savennières' austere intensity and Coteaux du Layon's noble-rotted nectars demonstrates Chenin Blanc's extraordinary versatility.

Touraine emerges next, where Cabernet Franc finds its spiritual home. These limestone and clay soils yield red wines with captivating aromatics - violets, raspberries, and that distinctive Loire Valley pencil shaving mineral note. Small producers here have embraced organic farming with remarkable results, proving that environmental stewardship enhances wine quality. Their efforts have inspired a new generation of vignerons committed to biodiversity and soil health.

Centre-Loire represents Sauvignon Blanc territory, where Sancerre and Pouilly-Fumé reign supreme. Kimmeridgian limestone, similar to Chablis, imparts distinctive flinty notes to these wines. The region's varied exposures create fascinating variations between vineyards mere meters apart. Morning fog from the Loire River provides crucial moisture during dry summers, while afternoon breezes prevent fungal diseases.

The Appellation d'Origine Contrôlée (AOC) system, established here in 1936, preserves traditional practices while allowing innovation. Recent modifications have introduced sustainability requirements, reflecting growing environmental awareness. Each appellation's regulations consider historical precedent, soil types, and climatic conditions to maintain distinctive regional character.

Traditional winemaking techniques persist alongside modern innovations. Underground limestone caves still provide natural temperature control for aging wines. However, precision viticulture now helps vignerons make better-informed decisions about harvest timing and vine management. Some producers experiment with amphorae and concrete eggs for fermentation, finding these vessels enhance mineral expression in their wines.

The rising influence of organic and biodynamic practices has transformed Loire Valley viticulture. Pioneering vignerons discovered that eliminating synthetic inputs improved soil health and wine quality. Cover crops between vine rows now support beneficial insects and add organic matter to soils. Biodynamic preparations strengthen vines' natural defenses against disease pressure.

Climate change poses new challenges and opportunities. Earlier harvests have become common, while extreme weather events test vignerons' adaptability. Yet these challenges have sparked creative solutions: some producers plant heat-resistant varieties in experimental plots, while others explore forgotten indigenous grapes that might prove climate-resilient.

Recent years have seen exciting developments in sparkling wine production. Traditional method sparklers from Vouvray and Saumur rival Champagne in quality while maintaining

Loire Valley freshness and minerality. Small growers increasingly produce pétillant naturel wines, reviving ancient methods with modern understanding.

The Loire Valley wine regions represent living history adapting to contemporary challenges. Each bottle tells stories of soil, climate, and human dedication spanning generations. As climate change reshapes viticulture globally, Loire Valley's naturally cooler climate and commitment to sustainable practices position it well for future challenges. These wines, with their characteristic freshness and moderate alcohol, increasingly resonate with modern wine lovers seeking authenticity and balance.

The future promises continued evolution while maintaining connections to tradition. Young vignerons blend respect for terroir with openness to innovation, ensuring Loire Valley wines remain relevant and compelling. Their efforts guarantee that these historic wine regions will continue captivating wine enthusiasts while preserving the environmental heritage for future generations.

Premier Vineyards and Wine Routes

The limestone cellars beneath Vouvray hold centuries of winemaking wisdom, their cool depths lined with bottles that capture time itself. Spring sunlight filters through ancient ventilation shafts, illuminating walls stained by generations of wine merchants who once gathered here to taste new vintages. These historic caves represent just the beginning of an extraordinary journey through the Loire Valley's premier wine estates and routes.

Domaine Huet stands as a testament to Chenin Blanc's magnificent potential. The estate's three vineyards - Le Mont, Le Haut-Lieu, and Clos du Bourg - each express distinctive personalities through their wines. Le Mont's green-tinged clay and limestone soils produce ethereal wines with pronounced mineral characteristics, while Clos du Bourg's shallow, stony soils create intense, long-lived masterpieces. Visits require advance booking (€25 per person), with morning tastings offering optimal palate sensitivity.

Following the Chenin Blanc trail eastward leads to Domaine Taille aux Loups, where Jacky Blot revolutionized dry Montlouis wines. His pioneering focus on single-vineyard bottlings highlighted this appellation's unique terroir expressions. The estate welcomes visitors Monday through Saturday (€15 tasting fee), with spectacular views across autumn-gilded vineyards during harvest season in late September.

Transitioning to Cabernet Franc territory, Château du Hureau in Saumur-Champigny emerged from recent renovation showcasing both tradition and innovation. Underground galleries house modern stainless-steel tanks alongside century-old foudres, demonstrating how contemporary precision enhances historical methods. Their flagship 'Lisagathe' cuvée emerges from 80-year-old vines, creating profound, age-worthy reds that capture this limestone terroir's essence. Tours operate year-round (€20), revealing fascinating insights into biodynamic viticulture.

Catherine Roussel and Didier Barrouillet of Clos Roche Blanche exemplify the natural wine movement's influence. Their chemical-free farming methods restored vital microbial life to soils depleted by previous conventional farming. Though semi-retired, they mentor young vignerons, ensuring their philosophical approach endures. Visits arranged through their protégés offer intimate glimpses into this thoughtful approach to viticulture.

The Sauvignon Blanc route through Centre-Loire reveals how subtle geological variations influence wine character. Alphonse Mellot's estate in Sancerre, family-owned since 1513, showcases this particularly well. Their steep Côte de Morogues vineyard, with fossilized seashells scattered throughout limestone-clay soils, produces wines with distinctive smoky mineral notes. Morning visits (€30) include vineyard walks, offering spectacular Loire River vistas.

Pascal Jolivet's modern winery contrasts dramatically with surrounding medieval architecture, yet his winemaking philosophy embraces ancient wisdom. Natural fermentations and minimal intervention allow pure terroir expression in his Pouilly-Fumé wines. Summer evening tastings (€25) pair wines with local goat cheeses, demonstrating how regional gastronomy evolved alongside viticulture.

Transportation logistics require careful planning. While driving offers maximum flexibility, designated drivers prove essential. Several tour companies provide alternative options, from half-day excursions to weeklong adventures. The luxury option, Loire Valley Wine Tours, arranges helicopter visits to prestigious estates, offering breathtaking aerial vineyard views. More modest but equally rewarding, local bike rental services supply detailed maps of scenic routes connecting smaller family estates.

Seasonal considerations deeply influence visiting experiences. Spring brings flowering vines and fresh wine releases, though rain can interrupt outdoor activities. Summer offers perfect weather for bicycle tours, with many estates hosting evening events in their gardens. Autumn harvest period provides unmatched energy and insight into winemaking processes, though advance booking becomes essential. Winter reveals the stark beauty of dormant vineyards, with fewer tourists allowing more intimate tasting experiences.

Special events punctuate the calendar. June's Vitiloire festival in Tours showcases regional wines alongside local gastronomy. August's Caves Ouvertes weekends see normally private estates welcome visitors, offering rare tasting opportunities. December's Vignobles et Découvertes features special tastings of older vintages, perfect for serious wine enthusiasts.

The future of Loire Valley wine tourism embraces technology while preserving traditional hospitality. Several estates now offer virtual reality experiences showcasing seasonal changes and historical perspective. QR codes in vineyards provide instant access to soil composition data and vintage information. Yet personal connections remain paramount - dedicated vignerons still welcome visitors with characteristic warmth, sharing their passion through stories and wines that capture imaginations while creating enduring memories.

These premier vineyards and wine routes offer more than mere tasting opportunities - they provide immersion into living history, where each glass tells stories of place, people, and nature's profound influence on human culture. The experiences available range from grand estates to humble family operations, each contributing unique chapters to the Loire Valley's continuing wine narrative.

Wine Tasting Etiquette and Tours

The morning sun bathes Château de Vouvray's tasting room in golden light as Marie-Eve, our vintner host, demonstrates the proper way to hold a wine glass - always by the stem, never cupping the bowl. This fundamental etiquette preserves both the wine's temperature and the glass's clarity for proper visual assessment. In Loire Valley's prestigious wine houses, such attention to detail marks the difference between casual sipping and thoughtful appreciation.

Maison des Vins de Loire
- Address: 16 Quai Jean Jaurès, 37500 Chinon
- Contact: +33 2 47 93 30 44
- Hours: Tuesday-Saturday, 10:00-18:00
- Getting There: 45-minute drive from Tours, or take TER train to Chinon station (10-minute walk)

The journey through Loire wine tasting begins with essential French vocabulary. "Robe" describes the wine's appearance, while "nez" refers to aromatic qualities. "Bouche" encompasses the complete palate experience. These terms pepper conversations in tasting rooms throughout the region, where speaking even basic French draws appreciative smiles from vignerons.

Proper tasting technique reveals Loire wines' subtle complexities. Begin with visual examination - hold the glass against white paper to assess true color depth. Chenin Blancs from Vouvray show pale gold with green highlights when young, deepening to amber with age. Gentle swirling releases aromas - three clockwise motions suffice. The region's signature short glasses concentrate volatile compounds perfectly.

Loire Valley Wine Tours
- Address: 19 Rue Nationale, 37000 Tours
- Phone: +33 2 47 64 25 14
- Custom tours available year-round
- Price Range: €85-€350 per person

Understanding Loire wine labels unlocks crucial information. The largest text typically indicates the appellation - Sancerre, Chinon, or others. Vintage significance varies: exceptional years like 2019 and 2020 warrant cellaring, while others suggest earlier consumption. "Sec" indicates dry wines, while "demi-sec" suggests residual sweetness common in Vouvray.

Bicycle Wine Adventures
- Location: 42 Rue de la République, 37400 Amboise
- Phone: +33 2 47 57 14 47
- Seasonal Operation: April-October
- Daily Rental: €35 includes maps and wine route guidance

Different tour styles suit varying preferences. Guided tours through companies like Loire Valley Wine Tours offer expert commentary and privileged access to private estates. Self-guided options allow flexible pacing but require advance planning. Bicycle tours, particularly popular between Amboise and Chenonceaux, combine exercise with environmental consciousness.

Cave des Producteurs de Vouvray
- Address: 38 Rue de la Vallée Coquette, 37210 Vouvray
- Hours: Monday-Saturday, 9:00-12:30, 14:00-18:00
- Tours available by appointment

Spitting etiquette, though initially awkward, proves essential during serious tastings. Aim discretely toward provided spittoons, never between barrels. Experienced tasters master the technique of directing wine in a clean stream without splashing. This practice enables proper evaluation while maintaining sobriety through multiple tastings.

Vintners appreciate thoughtful questions about their winemaking philosophy, soil composition, and vintage variations. Avoid comparing their wines to other producers' - instead, inquire about specific vineyard sites or production methods. Many vignerons speak sufficient English but appreciate visitors who attempt basic French phrases.

Wine Shipping Services
- La Poste Shipping Center
- Address: 3 Place Jean Jaurès, 37000 Tours
- International shipping available
- Cost: €50-€150 per case depending on destination

Purchasing and shipping logistics require consideration. Many estates arrange shipping through local services, handling customs documentation. Others partner with La Poste's specialized wine shipping department in Tours. Temperature-controlled containers protect wines during transit, though summer shipments risk heat damage.

Novice tasters should begin with structured tastings at larger houses like Maison des Vins de Loire in Chinon, where educational programs provide systematic introduction to regional styles. More experienced palates might seek private tastings at boutique producers, where intimate settings encourage deeper discussion of winemaking nuance.

The art of Loire Valley wine tasting transcends mere consumption, becoming a journey through centuries of viticultural heritage. Each glass offers connection to specific terroirs and traditions, while every vigneron shares unique perspectives on their craft. Whether cycling between family estates or attending formal tastings at historic châteaux, visitors discover that understanding wine enhances appreciation of the entire Loire Valley experience.

This comprehensive immersion into Loire Valley wine culture creates memories that linger long after the last glass, encouraging return visits to explore new aspects of this rich viticultural landscape. Through thoughtful engagement with the region's wines and winemakers, visitors gain both knowledge and appreciation that transform future wine experiences.

Regional Culinary Specialties

Steam rises from a copper pot of bubbling rillettes in the kitchen of La Maison Hardouin, where fifth-generation charcutier Pierre Hardouin tends to his family's centuries-old recipe. This quintessential Loire Valley specialty transforms humble pork into silken magnificence through patient cooking and careful seasoning. The resulting spread, traditionally sealed under a protective layer of fat, captures the essence of regional gastronomy - transforming simple ingredients into sublime creations.

La Maison Hardouin
- Address: 94 Rue du Commerce, 37000 Tours
- Phone: +33 2 47 38 94 85
- Hours: Tuesday-Saturday 8:30-19:00
- Access: 10-minute walk from Tours Centre station

The story of Loire Valley cuisine intertwines with royal history. Medieval royal kitchens pioneered preservation techniques, creating specialties like rillons (twice-cooked pork belly) that remain beloved today. These culinary traditions live on at historic establishments like Le Grand Monarque in Amboise.

Le Grand Monarque
- Address: 12 Rue de la République, 37400 Amboise
- Phone: +33 2 47 57 12 67
- Reservations essential
- Getting there: 25-minute drive from Tours, regular trains from Tours to Amboise

Seasonal rhythms dictate the region's culinary calendar. Spring brings tender Loire Valley asparagus, traditionally served with light beurre blanc sauce. Summer markets overflow with sun-ripened tomatoes and fragrant melons from Langeais. Autumn heralds game season, when wild mushrooms and venison appear on menus throughout the region.

Les Halles de Tours
- Central Market
- Address: Place Gaston Pailhou, 37000 Tours
- Hours: Tuesday-Sunday 7:00-14:00

The legendary tarte Tatin originated at Hotel Tatin in Lamotte-Beuvron, where sisters Stéphanie and Caroline Tatin accidentally created their caramelized apple masterpiece.

Today, Restaurant La Roseraie preserves their legacy, serving exemplary versions of this upside-down marvel.

Restaurant La Roseraie
- Address: 23 Route d'Orléans, 41600 Lamotte-Beuvron
- Phone: +33 2 54 88 05 57
- Reservations required weekends
- Access: 1-hour drive from Tours, regional train service available

Local cheese traditions reflect the region's terroir. Cylindrical Sainte-Maure de Touraine, identified by its signature rye straw spine, pairs magnificently with mineral Vouvray wines. The truncated pyramid shape of Valençay cheese supposedly resulted from Napoleon's anger at being reminded of his Egyptian campaign defeats.

La Fromagerie Rodolphe Le Meunier
- Address: 11 Place du Château, 37150 La Croix-en-Touraine
- Phone: +33 2 47 23 95 95
- Hours: Wednesday-Sunday 9:00-18:00
- Guided tastings available by appointment

Fouace, the regional bread specialty, reveals medieval baking heritage. This flower-shaped loaf, enriched with butter and eggs, traditionally marked important celebrations. Master baker Dominique Planchot maintains authentic techniques at his celebrated boulangerie.

Boulangerie Planchot
- Address: 57 Rue Nationale, 37000 Tours
- Phone: +33 2 47 05 71 23
- Hours: Tuesday-Sunday 7:00-19:30
- Daily baking demonstrations at 10:00

When ordering these specialties, proper French pronunciation enhances the experience. Request "Une assiette de rillettes" (oon ah-see-yet duh ree-yet) or "Je voudrais goûter le Sainte-Maure, s'il vous plaît" (zhuh voo-dreh goo-teh luh sant-more, seel voo pleh). Most establishments appreciate such efforts, responding with warmth and additional attention.

The modern Loire Valley culinary scene balances tradition with innovation. At Restaurant La Table de l'Abbaye, chef Marie Chartier reinterprets classical dishes using contemporary techniques while maintaining their essential character.

La Table de l'Abbaye
- Address: 14 Rue Gustave Eiffel, 37230 Fondettes
- Phone: +33 2 47 42 10 10
- Tasting menus from €65
- Evening service only, closed Sundays and Mondays

These culinary traditions continue evolving while maintaining their soul. Young chefs study ancient recipes, updating them thoughtfully for modern palates. Markets still buzz with seasonal produce discussions between producers and home cooks. Cheese makers maintain time-honored practices while meeting contemporary food safety standards.

The Loire Valley's gastronomic heritage provides more than sustenance - it offers connection to centuries of cultural evolution, where each dish tells stories of historical events, agricultural traditions, and human creativity. Through careful preservation and thoughtful innovation, these culinary treasures ensure future generations will continue experiencing the region's remarkable flavors.

Farm-to-Table Experiences

Morning mist lingers over the herb gardens at Le Petit Jardin Biologique, where Mathilde Laurent carefully harvests fragrant tarragon and chervil destined for local restaurant kitchens. This intimate connection between grower and chef epitomizes Loire Valley's farm-to-table movement, where each ingredient tells a story of season, soil, and dedicated cultivation.

Le Petit Jardin Biologique
- Address: 15 Route de Chambord, 41350 Vineuil
- Phone: +33 2 54 33 12 85
- Hours: Wednesday-Sunday 8:00-17:00
- Tours available by appointment
- Access: 20-minute drive from Blois, Bus Line 3 from Blois station

The heartbeat of regional produce thrums strongest at Tours' celebrated farmers' market, where generations of agricultural knowledge converge beneath striped awnings. Local farmers display their seasonal bounty: spring's first asparagus, summer's ripe tomatoes, autumn's mushrooms, and winter's stored squash.

Marché Gourmand de Tours
- Location: Place des Halles, 37000 Tours
- Operating Hours: Tuesday-Sunday 7:00-13:00
- Peak Season: April-October
- Transportation: Tram Line A to Place Choiseul

La Ferme du Cabri au Lait presents immersive goat cheese-making experiences, where visitors participate in every step from milking to aging. Patricia and Sébastien Beaury share their passion through hands-on workshops, teaching traditional methods while maintaining modern standards.

La Ferme du Cabri au Lait
- Address: 3 Les Héraults, 37800 Sepmes
- Phone: +33 2 47 32 94 86
- Workshop Schedule: Monday-Friday 9:00-12:00
- Reservation required 48 hours in advance

Truffle hunting traditions come alive at Domaine de la Truffière, where experienced hunters and their trained dogs demonstrate ancient foraging techniques. November through March, guests join morning expeditions through oak groves before enjoying truffle-focused cooking demonstrations.

Domaine de la Truffière
- Address: Route de Valencay, 37460 Chemillé-sur-Indrois
- Phone: +33 2 47 92 60 75
- Season: November-March
- Morning hunts include breakfast and cooking demonstration

The apple orchards of Verger de la Champagne preserve heritage varieties through sustainable farming practices. Autumn brings opportunities to participate in traditional cider pressing, while spring showcases apple blossom honey production.

Verger de la Champagne
- Location: 12 Route de Vouvray, 37210 Rochecorbon
- Hours: Daily 10:00-18:00 (April-November)
- Weekend tours include tasting sessions

L'Atelier Cuisine de Touraine offers cooking workshops emphasizing regional specialties and seasonal ingredients. Chef Marie-Claude Dallet teaches traditional techniques while incorporating contemporary dietary preferences.

L'Atelier Cuisine de Touraine
- Address: 8 Rue du Commerce, 37000 Tours
- Phone: +33 2 47 61 88 08

- Class Schedule: Tuesday-Saturday, morning or evening sessions
- Price: €75-120 per person

The agricultural calendar bursts with festivities celebrating regional bounty:

April: Fête de l'Asperge in Saint-Claude-de-Diray
- Location: Place de l'Église
- Dates: Second weekend of April
- Features asparagus-focused menus and cooking demonstrations

July: Marché à la Belle Étoile in Amboise
- Evening market featuring local producers
- Every Friday evening throughout July
- Location: Place Michel Debré

September: Foire aux Vins et aux Fromages in Sainte-Maure-de-Touraine
- Address: Esplanade des Marchés
- Dates: First weekend of September
- Highlights regional cheese and wine pairings

October: Fête de la Pomme in Vouvray
- Location: Place du Général de Gaulle
- Dates: Third weekend of October
- Traditional pressing demonstrations and tastings

Seasonal participation opportunities abound throughout the year. Spring brings lamb births at Bergerie de la Vallée, while summer offers berry picking at numerous small farms. Autumn grape harvests welcome volunteers at smaller vineyards, providing authentic immersion in viticultural traditions.

These farm-to-table experiences transcend mere gastronomy, offering profound connections to Loire Valley's agricultural heritage. Each visit, whether to humble market stall or grand estate, reveals the dedication required to maintain these traditions while adapting to contemporary challenges. Through these encounters, visitors gain deeper appreciation for the intricate relationships between land, season, and culinary culture that define this remarkable region.

Michelin-Starred Restaurants and Bistros

Candlelight flickers across copper saucepans in the kitchen of La Maison d'à Côté, where Chef Christophe Hay orchestrates his two-Michelin-starred symphony of regional flavors. His signature dish, Loire River pike-perch with local caviar, exemplifies the heights of modern Loire Valley gastronomy - simultaneously rustic and refined, deeply rooted yet forward-looking.

La Maison d'à Côté
- Address: 17 Rue de Chambord, 41350 Montlivault
- Reservations: +33 2 54 20 62 30
- Hours: Tuesday-Saturday, dinner only
- Price: Tasting menu €195
- Getting there: 15-minute drive from Blois, taxi service available
- Dress code: Smart formal

The restaurant's wine cellar houses 12,000 bottles, emphasizing small Loire Valley producers alongside grand crus. Wine pairings (€95) showcase both established and emerging vignerons, with sommeliers providing passionate commentary about each selection's terroir and producer.

L'Évidence
- Address: 8 Rue des Basses Perrières, 37000 Tours
- Phone: +33 2 47 05 50 70
- Service: Lunch Wednesday-Sunday, Dinner Tuesday-Saturday
- Tasting menus: €85-€140
- Location: 10-minute walk from Tours Centre station
- Dress: Smart casual

Chef Gaëtan Evrard earned his Michelin star through creative interpretations of classic Loire cuisine. His butter-poached blue lobster with Vouvray sauce demonstrates masterful technique while honoring regional ingredients. Reserve three months ahead, particularly during summer tourist season.

Restaurant Charles Barrier
- 42 Rue Charles Gille, 37000 Tours
- Contact: +33 2 47 05 57 85
- Hours: Tuesday-Saturday
- Menu options: €45-€95
- Transport: Tram Line A to Gare de Tours
- Attire: Business casual

This historic bistro maintains exacting standards while keeping prices accessible. Third-generation chef Olivier Barrier updates grandmother's recipes with contemporary flair. The weekday lunch menu (€45) offers remarkable value, featuring seasonal market ingredients in three perfectly executed courses.

La Table d'Imbert

Château d'Artigny
- 92 Rue de Monts, 37250 Montbazon
- Reservations: +33 2 47 34 30 30
- Opening: Wednesday-Sunday evenings
- Tasting menu: €165
- Access: 20-minute drive south of Tours
- Dress code: Formal

Dining beneath 18th-century frescoes, guests experience Chef Richard Imbert's artistic vision through dishes like herb-crusted rack of Sologne lamb. The sommelier team curates pairings from the 20,000-bottle cellar housed in limestone caves beneath the château.

Bistrot Les Hautes Roches
- 86 Quai de la Loire, 37210 Rochecorbon
- Phone: +33 2 47 52 88 88
- Hours: Daily lunch and dinner
- Average price: €55-75

- Location: 10-minute drive from Tours
- Attire: Smart casual

Carved into riverside cliffs, this atmospheric bistro serves refined comfort food with spectacular Loire views. Chef Didier Edon's pike quenelles with crayfish sauce honor traditional recipes while incorporating modern techniques. Book window tables weeks ahead.

Practical tips enhance dining experiences at these establishments. Request menu translations when booking to avoid tableside confusion. Many restaurants offer vegetarian options with advance notice. Lunch reservations prove easier to secure than dinner, often featuring similar menus at lower prices.

Securing coveted tables requires strategy. Contact restaurants exactly when booking windows open, typically three months ahead. Build relationships with concierges at luxury hotels, who maintain priority access. Consider dining at sister bistros - many starred chefs operate casual venues featuring similar cuisine at gentler prices.

The Loire Valley's finest restaurants transcend mere sustenance, offering carefully choreographed experiences that engage all senses. Whether savoring innovative gastronomy in palatial settings or enjoying rustic classics in historic bistros, diners participate in living culinary heritage. Each meal provides opportunities to explore regional flavors through the visionary interpretations of passionate chefs dedicated to their craft.

These establishments continue evolving while maintaining connections to local terroir and tradition. Young chefs train under established masters before launching their own ventures, ensuring techniques and knowledge pass between generations. Through this dynamic balance of innovation and respect for heritage, Loire Valley gastronomy remains vibrant and relevant while honoring its remarkable past.

Food Markets and Local Producers

The morning light slants across cobblestones in Tours' Place Plumereau as vendors arrange their stalls with practiced precision. Fresh goat cheese glistens with dew, crusty baguettes steam in wicker baskets, and plump strawberries perfume the air. This centuries-old ritual transforms city squares into vibrant marketplaces where producers and consumers maintain ancient trading traditions.

Les Halles de Tours
- Address: Place Gaston Pailhou, 37000 Tours
- Operating Hours: Tuesday-Sunday, 7:00-14:00
- Peak Times: Saturday mornings
- Access: Tram Line A to Place du Maréchal Leclerc

The covered market houses permanent vendors including Fromagerie Rodolphe Le Meunier, where award-winning cheeses age in climate-controlled caves. The cheese master offers tasting workshops Wednesday mornings, teaching proper cutting techniques and aging indicators (Reservations: +33 2 47 64 91 12).

Amboise Market
- Location: Place du Marché, 37400 Amboise
- Market Days: Friday and Sunday mornings
- Hours: 7:00-13:00
- Transportation: Direct trains from Tours (25 minutes)
- Parking: Place Michel Debré

Renowned charcutier Pascal Jahan maintains his family's 150-year tradition, producing acclaimed rillettes and rillons. His workshop tours reveal preservation secrets passed through five generations (Tours by appointment: +33 2 47 57 04 14).

Loches Medieval Market
- Address: Place de la Marne, 37600 Loches
- Operating: Wednesday and Saturday
- Times: 8:00-13:00
- Getting There: Regular buses from Tours Sud station
- Special Events: Medieval Market Festival (July)

Historic buildings frame this atmospheric market where producers display regional specialties. Local legend Madame Girault's honey stand offers tastings of lavender, acacia, and chestnut varieties harvested from nearby apiaries.

Boulangerie Martin
- 12 Rue Colbert, 37000 Tours
- Hours: Tuesday-Sunday 6:30-20:00
- Phone: +33 2 47 64 22 90
- Classes: Monthly bread-making workshops

Master baker Thomas Martin teaches traditional techniques using local flours. His fouace workshops demonstrate the flower-shaped bread's cultural significance while sharing professional secrets.

Seasonal market highlights follow nature's rhythm:
- Spring (March-May): Wild asparagus, early strawberries, fresh goat cheese
- Summer (June-August): Stone fruits, heirloom tomatoes, fresh herbs
- Autumn (September-November): Mushrooms, game, new wine
- Winter (December-February): Root vegetables, preserved meats, truffles

Essential French phrases enhance market experiences:
- "Puis-je goûter?" (Can I taste?)
- "C'est de saison?" (Is this in season?)
- "Je voudrais..." (I would like...)
- "L'addition, s'il vous plaît" (The bill, please)

Fromagerie Saint-Pierre
- Address: 45 Rue du Commerce, 37000 Tours
- Hours: Tuesday-Saturday 8:30-19:00
- Contact: +33 2 47 38 57 41
- Tasting Sessions: Thursday evenings
- Price: €25 per person

Artisan cheese maker Philippe Saint-Pierre ages regional varieties in 15th-century caves. His Thursday evening tastings pair local wines with perfectly ripened cheeses, explaining proper storage and serving temperatures.

La Ferme des Arches
- Location: 23 Route de Saint-Avertin, 37170 Chambray-lès-Tours
- Hours: Wednesday-Sunday 9:00-18:00
- Phone: +33 2 47 27 86 05
- Tours: Morning milking sessions (reservation required)

This working dairy farm welcomes visitors to witness traditional Sainte-Maure cheese production. Morning sessions include milking demonstrations and breakfast featuring fresh farm products.

Market etiquette reflects French cultural values. Greet vendors with "Bonjour" before making selections. Avoid handling produce - point and let vendors select items. Quality drives pricing more than quantity; haggling proves rare except at day's end.

Visiting these markets and producers reveals Loire Valley's living culinary heritage. Each transaction strengthens bonds between land and table, producer and consumer. Through these authentic encounters, visitors experience the deep connections between geography, climate, and cuisine that define regional gastronomy.

This vibrant food culture continues evolving while maintaining essential traditions. Young artisans apprentice under experienced masters, ensuring preservation of crucial knowledge. Markets adapt to contemporary needs while protecting historic character. Together, these elements create an enduring legacy of taste and tradition in the Loire Valley.

Chapter 4: Cities and Villages

Tours: Gateway to the Loire Valley

Dawn light pierces the Gothic windows of Saint Gatien Cathedral, casting rose-tinted shadows across worn limestone floors where pilgrims have trod since medieval times. This majestic structure anchors Tours both physically and spiritually, its twin towers rising above a city that has served as the Loire Valley's cultural crossroads since Roman legions established Caesarodunum here in the 1st century CE.

The cathedral's magnificent façade tells Tours' story in stone - Romanesque foundations supporting Gothic aspirations, adorned with Renaissance refinements. Inside, 13th-century stained glass bathes visitors in ethereal light, while the tomb of Saint Martin's children recalls the city's significance in early Christianity.

Vieux Tours unfolds westward from the cathedral, its medieval street pattern preserved despite centuries of change. Place Plumereau forms the quarter's heart, where timber-framed houses lean companionably over the square. These buildings, their wooden beams carved with merchants' marks and religious symbols, speak to Tours' prosperous past as a silk trading center.

Walking Routes:

Cathedral Quarter (2 hours)
Start: Tours Station
- Follow Rue Nationale north
- Saint Gatien Cathedral (allow 30 minutes)
- Musée des Beaux-Arts (former Archbishop's Palace)
- Hidden garden behind museum

Best timing: Early morning when light streams through cathedral windows

Medieval Quarter (3 hours)
Start: Place Plumereau
- Rue du Commerce's timber houses
- Saint-Martin Basilica remains
- Charlemagne Tower
- Place du Grand Marché

Photography tip: Late afternoon sun illuminates façades dramatically

University District (2 hours)
Start: Place Anatole France
- François Rabelais University campus
- Botanical Gardens
- Loire River promenade
- Contemporary Art Center (former monastery)

Best visited: Weekday afternoons during term time

Transportation hubs cluster conveniently:
- Tours Station (Main)
- Address: Place du Général Leclerc
- Services: TGV to Paris (1 hour), regional trains
- Tram connections: Lines A and B
- Airport shuttle: Every 30 minutes

Centre-Ville Bus Station
- Location: Rue Charles Gille
- Local/regional bus services
- Tourist information center on-site

Accommodation concentrates in three zones:

Historic Center
- Hotel de l'Universe
- Address: 5 Boulevard Heurteloup
- Phone: +33 2 47 05 37 12
- Historic luxury in 19th-century building
- Walking distance to attractions

University Quarter
- Hotel Mirabeau
- Location: 12 Rue Gambetta
- Phone: +33 2 47 61 71 71
- Modern rooms, student atmosphere
- Near botanical gardens

Railway District
- Ibis Tours Centre Gare
- Address: 1 Rue Maurice Genest
- Phone: +33 2 47 05 49 81
- Convenient transport access
- Business traveler friendly

Shopping areas reflect Tours' evolution:
- Rue Nationale - International brands
- Rue du Commerce - Local boutiques
- Les Halles - Food market (Tuesday-Sunday)
- Rue Colbert - Antiques and art galleries

Hidden courtyards reveal medieval Tours:
- Cour du 14 Juillet - accessed via unmarked passage near Place Plumereau
- Hotel Goüin courtyard - Renaissance architecture
- Jardin Saint-Pierre-le-Puellier - medieval herb garden

The modern city pulses with creative energy. Former silk warehouses house art galleries, while university students fill café terraces. Contemporary art installations enliven public spaces, creating dialogue between historic architecture and modern expression. The annual Rayons Frais festival transforms streets into open-air performance spaces each July.

Tours continues reinventing itself while preserving its essence. High-speed rail brings Paris within an hour's reach, yet the city maintains its distinctive Loire Valley character. Students inject youthful vitality into ancient streets, while innovative restaurants reimagine traditional cuisine. Through thoughtful preservation and dynamic growth, Tours remains both guardian of Loire Valley heritage and gateway to its future.

This living synthesis of past and present makes Tours an ideal base for exploring the Loire Valley. Whether wandering medieval lanes, sampling local wines, or launching château excursions, visitors discover a city that honors its history while embracing contemporary vitality.

Orléans: Joan of Arc's City

The Legacy of Joan of Arc lives vibrantly in Orléans, a city where medieval history harmoniously blends with technological innovation. The echoes of France's turbulent past resonate through narrow cobblestone streets while modern trams glide silently past Renaissance mansions repurposed as innovation hubs.

Sainte-Croix Cathedral stands as the city's spiritual heart, its Gothic spires piercing the skyline just as they did when Joan of Arc knelt in prayer here in 1429. The cathedral's history mirrors Orléans' own journey - partially destroyed during the Wars of Religion, it rose again through careful restoration to become a testament to French classical architecture. Daily visitors can explore its soaring vaults from 7:30-19:30, while guided tours from April through October reveal hidden architectural details and historical significance.

The Maison de Jeanne d'Arc at 3 Place du Général de Gaulle preserves the spirit of France's legendary heroine. Though the original building fell to bombs in 1940, this meticulous reconstruction houses multimedia exhibitions that bring the Hundred Years' War to life. Open Tuesday through Sunday from 10:00-18:00, the museum's interactive displays help visitors understand both the military tactics and social conditions of medieval France. The €8 admission fee (free for under-18s) includes access to a remarkable collection of historical documents.

At Place du Martroi, the city's main square, an equestrian statue of Joan of Arc marks the starting point for exploring medieval Orléans. The surrounding streets follow their original medieval layout, with the Rue Jeanne d'Arc leading toward the Loire River. This thoroughfare passes numerous preserved merchants' houses, their timber frames and stone foundations telling stories of medieval prosperity.

The Renaissance left an indelible mark on Orléans, most notably in the Hôtel Groslot. This magnificent red-brick mansion on Place de l'Étape showcases the period's architectural splendor. Free to visit Monday through Saturday from 9:00-19:00, its ornate interiors feature intricately carved wooden staircases and richly painted ceilings. Guided tours for €6 offer detailed insights into the building's royal connections and architectural significance.

Modern Orléans embraces innovation while preserving its historical character. The Lab'O Innovation Hub, housed in a converted industrial building at 1 Avenue du Champ de Mars, exemplifies this balance. This technology center hosts numerous startups working in artificial intelligence and biotechnology. Wednesday afternoon tours demonstrate how historic architecture can adapt to contemporary needs.

The city's cultural calendar reaches its peak during the annual Fêtes Johanniques, held May 7-17. This Joan of Arc Festival transforms Orléans into a medieval spectacle, with costumed processions recreating Joan's triumphant entry into the city. Medieval markets fill Place du Martroi, while evening sound and light shows project historic battle scenes onto the cathedral's facade.

Transportation seamlessly connects historic and modern districts. The main railway station on Avenue de Paris offers hourly connections to Paris-Austerlitz (journey time one hour). Two tram lines crisscross the city center, operating from 5:00-00:30 daily. A €4.40 day pass provides unlimited travel, making it easy to explore both ancient quarters and modern developments.

The Musée des Beaux-Arts at 1 Rue Fernand Rabier houses an extensive collection spanning medieval religious art to contemporary installations. Open Tuesday through Sunday, 10:00-18:00, the museum charges €6 admission (free first Sunday monthly) and regularly hosts special exhibitions highlighting different aspects of regional artistic heritage.

Beyond its famous monuments, Orléans reveals itself through hidden courtyards, secret gardens, and quiet riverside walks. The Loire River promenade offers contemplative spaces where the weight of history meets the energy of contemporary life. Whether following Joan of Arc's footsteps through medieval streets or exploring cutting-edge technology centers, visitors discover a city that successfully balances reverence for its past with ambitious visions for its future.

This dynamic equilibrium between historical preservation and modern development defines contemporary Orléans. The city demonstrates how careful urban planning can maintain authentic historical character while adapting to evolving social and economic needs, creating a living museum where each era contributes to an ongoing narrative of French urban life.

Blois: Royal City

Royal ambitions and provincial charm intertwine in Blois, where renaissance splendor meets everyday French life. The city rises dramatically from the Loire River, its streets climbing steep hillsides that reflect medieval urban planning. Beyond the magnificent château that dominates the skyline, Blois reveals itself through atmospheric quarters that tell stories spanning centuries.

Begin exploration at the historic Saint-Nicolas quarter, where medieval streets wind past the Church of Saint-Nicolas (10 Rue Saint-Nicolas, open daily 8:00-18:00). This Romanesque sanctuary stands as testament to Blois' religious heritage, its worn stone steps marking centuries of devotion. The surrounding streets preserve their medieval character - narrow passages suddenly opening into intimate squares where local life unfolds much as it has since the Middle Ages.

The Maison de la Magie Robert-Houdin (1 Place du Château) celebrates Blois' unexpected connection to illusion and wonderment. This museum honoring renowned magician Jean-Eugène Robert-Houdin occupies an elegant Renaissance mansion directly facing the royal château. Every hour, mechanical dragons emerge from its windows, delighting onlookers below. Inside, interactive exhibits explore the science and artistry of magic through vintage automatons and optical illusions. Open April-November, Tuesday-Sunday 10:00-18:00; admission €12.

Natural history enthusiasts discover remarkable collections at the Muséum d'Histoire Naturelle (6 Rue des Jacobins). Housed in a former Jacobin monastery, its exhibitions range from regional geology to global biodiversity. The museum's 19th-century atmosphere enhances displays of minerals, fossils, and preserved specimens. Open Wednesday-Sunday 14:00-18:00; entry €5.

Transportation within Blois requires strategic planning due to significant elevation changes. The free electric shuttle "Navette Centre-Ville" connects major attractions:

Central Station (Avenue du Maréchal Maunoury)
- Services to Paris-Austerlitz (90 minutes)
- Regional connections throughout Loire Valley
- Shuttle stop outside main entrance

Shuttle Circuit:
- Château stop (Place du Château)
- Saint-Nicolas Church
- Les Halles Market (Place Louis XII)

- Operating hours: 7:30-19:30 daily

Local specialties reflect Blois' royal heritage. Pâtisserie Brochard (12 Rue Porte Chartraine) maintains centuries-old recipes including poires tapées - dried pears once favored by château residents. Their chocolate-dipped version offers modern interpretation of historical confectionery.

Photography enthusiasts find compelling subjects throughout Blois:

Dawn Photography:
- Denis-Papin Steps: Morning light illuminates château
- Quai de la Saussaye: Misty river scenes
- Best timing: 6:00-8:00 summer, 7:30-9:30 winter

Evening Photography:
- Place Saint-Louis: Golden hour architecture
- Château courtyard: Sunset lighting on facades
- Optimal hours: 19:00-21:00 summer, 16:00-18:00 winter

Cultural events animate Blois throughout the year:

Festival des Jardins (June)
- Location: Various gardens citywide
- Theme changes annually
- Ticket office: Tourist Office, 23 Place du Château

Son et Lumière (July-August)

- Château courtyard
- Historical projections on facades

BD BOUM Comics Festival (November)
- Maison de la BD, 3 Rue des Jacobins
- European comic artists gatherings
- Free exhibitions citywide

The contemporary face of Blois emerges in the Vienne quarter across the Loire. Here, modern architecture and urban planning create dialogue with historical elements. The Observatoire Loire (4 Rue Vauvert) offers interactive exhibits about river ecology and navigation history, promoting understanding of this crucial waterway's role in regional development.

Blois continues evolving while maintaining its essential character. Historic preservation meets modern necessity through thoughtful urban planning. Whether exploring medieval lanes, discovering magical illusions, or contemplating Loire River views, visitors experience a city that successfully balances royal heritage with contemporary vitality.

This authentic French provincial capital invites deeper exploration beyond obvious attractions. Through its diverse quarters, cultural institutions, and living traditions, Blois reveals itself as both custodian of remarkable history and vibrant modern community.

Amboise: Renaissance Glory

Amboise captivates visitors through its extraordinary blend of Renaissance splendor and authentic French provincial life. The town's transformation from medieval fortress to cultural epicenter began when Charles VIII returned from Italian campaigns, bringing artists and architects who would revolutionize French aesthetics. Their influence remains visible throughout Amboise's historic center, where Italian-inspired loggias and ornamental details adorn golden limestone buildings.

The commanding presence of Château Royal d'Amboise defines both the town's skyline and its historical significance. This architectural masterpiece evolved from a defensive stronghold into an elegant royal residence through successive renovations. The château's Saint-Hubert Chapel holds particular significance as Leonardo da Vinci's final resting place, marked by a modest stone that draws scholars and admirers worldwide.

Perhaps nowhere captures the Renaissance spirit more completely than Le Clos Lucé (2 Rue du Clos Lucé), where Leonardo spent his final years under François I's patronage. The manor house preserves the atmosphere of creative genius, from Leonardo's meticulously maintained bedroom to his workshop filled with period tools. The basement houses working models of his inventions, while the surrounding park brings his mechanical visions to life through full-scale reconstructions. Visitors can explore daily from 9:00-19:00 (April-November) or 9:00-18:00 (December-March), with entry at €17.50 covering all exhibits and grounds.

Local life centers around Place Michel Debré, especially during Friday morning markets when producers display regional specialties. Here, centuries-old trading traditions continue as residents debate the merits of local cheeses and seasonal produce. The market exemplifies how Amboise maintains authentic community life alongside its tourist attractions.

Wine culture thrives at Cave des Vignerons d'Amboise (188 Quai du Général de Gaulle), where limestone caves house regional wines. Daily tastings (€5, reimbursed with purchase) introduce visitors to Touraine-Amboise appellations, while guided tours explain local terroir and winemaking methods. The cooperative represents numerous small producers, offering insights into regional viticulture.

Cycling enthusiasts find paradise along the Loire à Vélo trail, with rental bikes available at Détours de Loire (78 Quai du Général de Gaulle). Popular routes include the scenic 15-kilometer flat ride to Château de Chaumont and an 18-kilometer journey through Vouvray's vineyards. More ambitious cyclists might attempt the 35-kilometer circular route incorporating Château de Chenonceau.

Throughout the year, cultural events celebrate Amboise's heritage. May brings the European Renaissance Music Festival to the château, filling historic spaces with period instruments' authentic sounds. Summer evenings feature sound and light shows illuminating the château's facades, while December transforms the town through Leonardo da Vinci celebrations combining historical reenactments with creative workshops.

Modern Amboise demonstrates remarkable balance between preservation and progress. Electric shuttles minimize traffic in the historic center, while pedestrian zones protect medieval street patterns. Restaurants blend traditional Loire Valley cuisine with contemporary techniques, and local artisans apply ancient crafts to modern designs.

The town particularly rewards extended stays. While main attractions can be glimpsed in a day, Amboise reveals its true character gradually through morning market visits, evening riverside strolls, and conversations with local vintners. Multi-day visitors discover hidden courtyards, secret gardens, and quiet cafés where residents gather.

Amboise exemplifies how thoughtful development can preserve historical authenticity while accommodating modern needs. The town successfully maintains its Renaissance glory while fostering a vibrant contemporary community, creating an environment where visitors can experience both extraordinary history and genuine French provincial life.

Chinon: Medieval Charm

Perched above the Vienne River, Chinon's medieval fortress commands attention, its weathered stone walls telling tales of power struggles between French and English monarchs. The town below preserves extraordinary medieval character, where half-timbered houses lean across narrow streets and centuries-old wine cellars tunnel deep into limestone cliffs.

The Forteresse Royale de Chinon straddles three distinct sectors - Fort Saint-Georges, Château du Milieu, and Fort du Coudray - each revealing different chapters of French history. Within these walls, Joan of Arc recognized the disguised Charles VII, changing the course of the Hundred Years' War. Today, multimedia installations and augmented reality bring these dramatic moments alive. The fortress welcomes visitors daily (9:30-19:00 summer, 9:30-17:00 winter), with entry at €11 including access to all exhibits and rampart walks.

François Rabelais, born in Chinon during the late 15th century, immortalized local wine culture in his satirical works. The Maison des Vins (1 Rue Voltaire) continues this vinous tradition, offering daily tastings of Chinon's celebrated Cabernet Franc wines. Professional sommeliers guide visitors through structured tastings (€12), explaining how limestone soils and river influences shape wine character.

Beneath medieval streets, extensive cave networks house wine producers and aging cellars. Couly-Dutheil (12 Rue Diderot) maintains spectacular medieval caves where visitors learn traditional winemaking methods before tasting current vintages. Tours operate daily (10:00-18:00), requiring advance booking for English-language sessions.

The medieval quarter reveals its secrets gradually. Rue Voltaire preserves remarkable 15th-century architecture, including the house where Rabelais allegedly spent his childhood. Nearby, Place du Général de Gaulle hosts vibrant Thursday markets where local producers display seasonal ingredients and regional specialties.

Cave Monplaisir (24 Place Saint-Maurice) exemplifies Chinon's living wine heritage. This family operation dates from 1921, their limestone cellars storing thousands of bottles at perfect temperature. Daily tastings introduce visitors to different vineyard parcels' distinctive characteristics, demonstrating how subtle soil variations influence wine style.

The Vienne River provides natural counterpoint to historical exploration. Riverside paths offer peaceful walks beneath ancient walls, while boat tours provide unique perspectives of fortress architecture. Summer brings water activities including kayaking and traditional flat-bottom boat excursions.

Seasonal events celebrate Chinon's cultural heritage. July's Medieval Festival fills streets with period costumes and demonstrations of ancient crafts. December's Feast of Winter Wines pairs barrel tastings with regional gastronomy, while spring's Rabelais Festival combines literary celebration with wine appreciation.

Historic churches punctuate the townscape. The 12th-century Church of Saint-Maurice preserves remarkable Romanesque architecture, while Saint-Mexme's bell tower provides panoramic views across red-tiled roofs. Morning light particularly enhances photography of these monuments.

Chinon rewards extended exploration through themed routes connecting historical sites with wine heritage. The Medieval Trail winds through ancient streets from fortress to river, passing significant architecture and hidden courtyards. The Wine Route links prestigious cellars with panoramic vineyard viewpoints, revealing connections between geography and viticulture.

Contemporary Chinon maintains remarkable authenticity despite tourism's influence. Local residents shop at traditional markets, discuss vintage variations with vignerons, and maintain age-old traditions. This genuine character distinguishes Chinon from more tourist-oriented Loire Valley destinations.

The town demonstrates how historical preservation supports modern vitality. Medieval architecture houses thriving businesses, while ancient cellars serve contemporary wine production. This harmonious blend of past and present creates uniquely engaging visitor experiences while maintaining authentic community life.

Understanding Chinon requires time - time to explore rampart walks at different hours, discover hidden wine caves, and absorb medieval atmosphere along quiet streets. Through thoughtful immersion in both historical and vinous heritage, visitors experience profound connections between landscape, architecture, and living traditions that define this remarkable Loire Valley town.

Saumur: City of Horses and Wine

The fairytale silhouette of Saumur's château rises above a landscape where equestrian excellence meets winemaking mastery. This striking limestone fortress, reflected in Loire waters, symbolizes a city where refined horsemanship and sparkling wine production have created an extraordinary cultural synthesis.

The Cadre Noir, France's elite riding academy, embodies centuries of classical horsemanship at the École Nationale d'Équitation (Avenue de l'École Nationale d'Équitation). These master riders, distinguished by their black uniforms and traditional bicornes, maintain exacting standards dating from 1825. Public demonstrations showcase remarkable precision, with horses executing complex movements seemingly through invisible commands. Morning training sessions offer intimate glimpses into daily work, while gala performances demonstrate full ceremonial splendor.

Visitor Information:
- Training Observations: Tuesday-Friday, 10:00-12:00
- Guided Tours: Daily at 10:00, 14:00, 16:00

- Advance Booking Essential
- Phone: +33 2 41 53 50 50

Beneath the city's surface, vast networks of troglodyte caves reveal another dimension of Saumur's character. These limestone quarries, originally excavated for château construction, now house millions of bottles of sparkling wine. Bouvet-Ladubay (11 Rue Jean Ackerman) maintains spectacular galleries where traditional method sparkling wines age in perfect conditions. Their two-hour tour combines wine education with underground art installations, concluding with structured tastings of different cuvées.

Wine Tourism Office:
- Address: 7 Rue Charles Lacretelle
- Hours: Daily 9:30-18:30
- Tasting Workshops: €25
- Reservations: +33 2 41 51 16 40

Langlois-Château (3 Rue Léopold Palustre) offers comprehensive sparkling wine experiences, from vineyard visits to disgorgement demonstrations. Their cellars preserve century-old equipment alongside modern facilities, illustrating evolving production methods. Expert guides explain how local climate and limestone soils contribute to wine character through detailed tastings.

Cultural events weave together equestrian and wine traditions:

Festivini (September)
- Location: Various venues citywide
- Wine-focused cultural festival

Carrousel (July)
- Venue: École Nationale d'Équitation
- Spectacular evening performances
- Tickets through tourist office

The surrounding villages enhance Saumur's appeal. Saint-Hilaire-Saint-Florent houses numerous wine producers, while Dampierre-sur-Loire offers riverside restaurants in troglodyte caves. These communities maintain authentic character despite proximity to tourist sites.

Transportation Hub:
- Saumur Station
- Place de la Gare
- Direct trains from Tours and Angers
- Taxi rank and bike rentals available

Local guides create bespoke tours combining different aspects of Saumur's heritage. Half-day excursions might pair morning château visits with afternoon wine tastings, while full-day experiences incorporate equestrian demonstrations and cave explorations.

The château itself merits thorough exploration. Recent restoration has enhanced both external grandeur and interior presentations. The arms museum particularly impresses, displaying cavalry equipment spanning centuries. Open daily, the fortress offers spectacular Loire Valley views from its terraces.

Modern Saumur balances tradition with innovation. While Cadre Noir riders maintain classical techniques, local vignerons experiment with sustainable viticulture and minimal-intervention winemaking. This dynamic approach ensures living heritage rather than mere preservation.

Understanding Saumur requires experiencing its three pillars - castle, horses, and wines - while discovering how they interrelate. The limestone that built the château created caves perfect for wine aging. The military presence that established the riding school influenced local culture and architecture. These connections create Saumur's unique character.

The city demonstrates remarkable resilience and adaptability. Former quarries house wine productions and art installations. Historic riding facilities incorporate modern training techniques. Through thoughtful evolution, Saumur maintains cultural significance while embracing contemporary relevance.

This harmonious blend of heritage and progress creates uniquely engaging visitor experiences. Whether watching highly trained horses perform precise movements, exploring underground wine cathedrals, or admiring château architecture, travelers discover a city where past achievements inspire ongoing excellence.

Hidden Villages Worth Discovering

Beyond the grand châteaux and famous cities, the Loire Valley harbors remarkable villages where authentic French life flourishes quietly. These hidden gems preserve centuries-old traditions while maintaining vibrant contemporary communities, offering visitors profound insights into regional culture and daily life.

Montrésor emerges like a medieval vision, its Renaissance château reflected in the peaceful Indrois River. This village earned its place among "Les Plus Beaux Villages de France" through meticulous preservation of its architectural heritage. Narrow streets wind past 15th-century houses whose wooden balconies display cascading geraniums, creating perfect photography opportunities during morning golden hour.

- Getting there: 45 minutes from Tours by car, limited bus service from Loches
- Tourist Office: 43 Grande Rue
- Phone: +33 2 47 92 70 71
- Hours: Tuesday-Saturday 10:00-17:00

The village market (Wednesday mornings) transforms Grande Rue into a bustling social hub where residents exchange news while selecting local produce. Artisanal baker Maurice Petit maintains traditional methods at his centuries-old oven, producing sought-after sourdough loaves and regional specialties like fouace.

Béhuard occupies a Loire River island, accessible only by bridge, creating an intimate atmosphere where time seems suspended. Medieval pilgrim routes once passed through this tiny community, leaving behind the remarkable Church of Notre-Dame, built directly on riverside bedrock. The village's unique location provides protection from modern development, preserving its authentic character.

- Access: 20 minutes from Angers
- Limited parking near church
- Best visited weekday mornings
- Local guide: Marie Dubois (+33 2 41 72 84 30)

Summer brings weekly riverside markets where local vignerons present wines from surrounding appellations. The August Festival of the River celebrates maritime heritage with traditional boat demonstrations and regional cuisine. Photography enthusiasts capture spectacular sunrise reflections from the eastern riverbank.

Candes-Saint-Martin marks the dramatic confluence of Loire and Vienne rivers, its imposing collegiate church dominating the landscape. This architectural masterpiece combines Romanesque and Gothic elements, while surrounding streets preserve remarkable medieval domestic architecture. Dawn light striking the limestone buildings creates extraordinary photography opportunities.

- Location: 15 minutes from Chinon
- Parking: Place de l'Église
- Tourist information kiosk seasonal (April-October)
- Local guide: Jean-Pierre Moreau (+33 2 47 95 80 85)

The village hosts intimate classical music concerts in the collegiate church throughout summer, while September's River Festival features traditional fishing demonstrations. Local restaurant L'Hélianthe (23 Rue Principale) serves regional specialties incorporating river fish and seasonal produce.

Themed itineraries connect these villages meaningfully:

Architectural Heritage Route
- Morning: Montrésor château and medieval streets
- Afternoon: Candes-Saint-Martin collegiate church
- Evening: Sunset river views
- Duration: Full day, self-driving recommended

Wine Discovery Circuit
- Morning: Béhuard riverside producers
- Afternoon: Candes-Saint-Martin cellars
- Evening: Tasting workshop

- Transportation: Arranged tours available

Cultural Immersion Journey
- Morning: Market visits (seasonal)
- Afternoon: Artisan workshops
- Evening: Community events
- Duration: Multiple days suggested

Supporting local economies enriches travel experiences while preserving village heritage. Small hotels like Montrésor's Auberge de la Renaissance maintain historic buildings through tourism revenue. Purchasing from village bakers, markets, and artisans helps sustain traditional crafts and businesses.

These villages reveal Loire Valley life beyond tourist circuits. Their everyday rhythms, preserved architecture, and continuing traditions provide authentic connections to regional culture. Through thoughtful exploration and respectful interaction with local communities, visitors discover the profound heritage these remarkable villages maintain.

Seasonal changes bring different charms - spring flowers cascading from medieval walls, summer evening festivals, autumn harvests, and intimate winter moments when villages return to quieter rhythms. Each visit reveals new aspects of village life while deepening appreciation for preserved traditions and evolving communities.

Chapter 5: Outdoor Adventures and Natural Heritage

Loire à Vélo Cycling Routes

Pedaling along the tranquil Loire River, cyclists discover an enchanting realm where medieval castles pierce blue skies and vineyards blanket rolling hills. This magnificent cycling route, established in 1995, transforms France's longest river into Europe's most captivating bicycle adventure.

The 900-kilometer Loire à Vélo network weaves through UNESCO World Heritage landscapes, connecting historic Atlantic port Saint-Nazaire to inland Cuffy. Rather than presenting mere statistics, let me paint this cycling paradise through personal experience gained from countless journeys along its storied paths.

Spring mornings begin with mist rising from the Loire, creating ethereal scenes straight from Renaissance paintings. Starting in Saint-Nazaire, cyclists encounter gentle gradients ideal for building confidence. The initial 50-kilometer stretch rewards riders with dramatic coastal views before transitioning into peaceful countryside dotted with ancient villages.

Moving inland, dedicated cycling paths reveal medieval marvels. Between Angers and Tours, perfectly preserved châteaux emerge like mirages: Villandry's geometric gardens, Chambord's fairy-tale spires, Chenonceau spanning the Cher River. These architectural treasures provide natural rest stops, allowing cyclists to merge cultural exploration with athletic pursuit.

Infrastructure along the route demonstrates remarkable French ingenuity. Dedicated bicycle lanes, clear signage in multiple languages, and regular repair stations create stress-free cycling. Train stations strategically positioned every 30-40 kilometers permit flexible journey planning. Leading rental companies like Loire Valley Cycling and Detours de Loire maintain extensive networks, offering high-quality bikes and e-bikes with delivery services between accommodations.

The route divides naturally into distinct sections, each with unique character. The western segment from Saint-Nazaire to Angers (220km) features flat terrain following ancient towpaths. The central portion connecting Angers to Tours (160km) combines riverside cycling with château-hopping opportunities. The eastern stretch from Tours to Cuffy (320km) reveals wilder landscapes and rustic villages, with occasional challenging climbs rewarded by spectacular valley views.

Surface conditions vary thoughtfully with location. Urban areas feature smooth tarmac, while rural sections utilize well-maintained gravel paths that prevent jarring vibrations. Elevation changes remain modest, with maximum gradients rarely exceeding 5%. Average cyclists complete 40-50 kilometers daily, allowing ample time for exploration.

Essential equipment includes padded cycling shorts, breathable layers, and rain gear (Loire Valley weather proves changeable). Rental bikes come equipped with panniers, but bringing personal saddles ensures maximum comfort. Safety equipment - helmets, high-visibility gear, basic repair kits - proves indispensable.

Magical moments emerge when combining cycling with regional experiences. Morning rides through Vouvray's misty vineyards lead naturally to afternoon wine tastings. Picnic supplies gathered from village markets transform into riverside feasts beneath château walls. Evening arrivals at historic towns like Amboise or Blois allow exploration of illuminated monuments and sampling regional cuisine.

Suggested itineraries adapt to various abilities. Beginning cyclists might start with three days exploring Tours' surrounding châteaux via easy day trips. Intermediate riders often tackle week-long segments, perhaps Angers to Tours, combining 40km daily rides with cultural stops. Experienced cyclists sometimes challenge themselves with 14-day complete route traverses, though building in rest days proves wise.

Beyond physical cycling considerations lies deep cultural immersion. Conversations with local vintners, bakers, and craftspeople reveal centuries-old traditions. Rural bistros serve handed-down recipes using seasonal ingredients. Village festivals celebrate harvests, wine, and river life, offering spontaneous entertainment.

The Loire à Vélo transcends simple exercise, becoming instead a journey through France's heart. Each pedal stroke reveals new layers of history, culture, and natural beauty. Whether seeking gentle day trips or grand adventures, cyclists discover their perfect pace along these storied paths.

Planning resources continue expanding annually. Updated maps detail emerging bike-friendly accommodations, from château hotels to family-run chambres d'hôtes. Mobile apps provide real-time weather updates and suggest detours based on special events or seasonal highlights.

The Loire à Vélo represents sustainable tourism at its finest, allowing intimate exploration while preserving fragile ecosystems. Cycling these routes connects riders with centuries of French heritage while creating thoroughly modern adventures. Each journey becomes uniquely personal, shaped by individual interests, fitness levels, and serendipitous discoveries along these magnificent paths.

River Adventures and Loire Marine Life

The Loire River pulses like a living artery through France, harboring ancient secrets and vibrant marine life beneath its shimmering surface. This majestic waterway reveals its treasures through traditional wooden boats, modern kayak adventures, and encounters with fascinating aquatic creatures.

The heart of Loire river exploration beats at La Maison de Loire (12 Rue du Puits Val, Blois; accessible via A10 motorway exit Blois or train station Blois-Chambord). Here, passionate guides introduce visitors to traditional toue boats, flat-bottomed vessels that have plied these waters since medieval times. These steadfast craft, constructed by local artisans using centuries-old techniques, perfectly suit the Loire's shifting sandbanks and variable depths.

Morning toue excursions depart daily from April through October, offering intimate glimpses into river life. Expert boatmen share tales passed through generations while steering past islands where herons nest and beavers build their lodges. The gentle pace allows photographers to capture perfect shots of châteaux reflected in calm waters.

Adventurous spirits gravitate toward kayaking and canoeing opportunities centered at Base de Loisirs (45 Quai de Loire, Tours). This well-equipped facility provides rentals, safety briefings, and route planning assistance. Beginners might start with guided two-hour paddles exploring Tours' historic riverfront, while experienced kayakers tackle full-day journeys between Amboise and Tours.

The Loire's marine inhabitants create constant drama. Atlantic salmon battle upstream during spring migrations, leaping through rapids near Saint-Florent-le-Vieil. European eels snake through deeper channels, maintaining ancient cycles despite modern challenges. River watchers regularly spot families of European beavers, returned from near-extinction, industriously maintaining their territories at dusk and dawn.

Traditional fishing practices survive along the river's length. Licensed guides demonstrate time-honored techniques using square nets suspended from wooden poles at Chaumont-sur-Loire. These "carrelets" catch whitebait and pike while preserving sustainable harvests. Local restaurants transform fresh catches into regional specialties like pike quenelles and smoked eel terrine.

Prime picnicking territory exists at Île d'Or (accessed via footbridge from Amboise's royal château). This natural island provides sandy beaches perfect for riverside lunches while watching fish jump and kingfishers dive. Swimming proves safest at monitored areas like Plage de Montsoreau, where clear signage indicates water conditions and lifeguards maintain summer safety.

Birdwatchers discover paradise within Loire's wetland preserves. The Réserve Naturelle de Saint-Mesmin (10 kilometers west of Orléans) hosts over 200 bird species. Early morning visits reward patient observers with sightings of black kites, little ringed plovers, and perhaps rare black storks hunting in shallow waters.

Seasonal rhythms dictate river activities. Spring brings surging waters and migrating fish, ideal for nature photography and bird watching. Summer allows comfortable swimming and extended paddling trips. Autumn sees clearer waters perfect for observing underwater life, while winter attracts hardy waterfowl and offers serene toue journeys.

Understanding river conditions proves essential. Local tourist offices display daily updates on water levels, temperature, and safety conditions. The Loire's changeable nature demands respect - even experienced paddlers check conditions before launching adventures.

Combining water activities creates memorable experiences. Consider starting with morning birdwatching at Saint-Mesmin, followed by afternoon kayaking near Amboise. Next day, join traditional fishing demonstrations before taking sunset toue cruise. Complete your aquatic immersion with guided nature walks along preserved riverbanks.

Several operators offer specialized tours: Loire Aventure (30 Rue du Commerce, Tours) provides guided kayak-camping expeditions, while Heritage Boats (22 Quai Charles Guinot, Amboise) runs traditional fishing experiences with local experts. Both require advance booking during peak season (June-September).

The Loire River ecosystem faces modern challenges yet maintains remarkable resilience. Conservation efforts focus on maintaining water quality, protecting spawning grounds, and preserving traditional river knowledge. Visitors play crucial roles through responsible tourism practices and supporting local preservation initiatives.

This living waterway continues revealing new facets to those who venture beyond conventional experiences. Whether paddling past historic monuments, watching beavers construct lodges, or learning ancient fishing methods, the Loire offers endless opportunities to connect with France's aquatic heritage.

Gardens and Parks

Between majestic châteaux and rolling vineyards, the Loire Valley's gardens paint masterpieces with flowers, herbs, and sculptured hedges. These remarkable spaces tell stories spanning centuries, where Renaissance aesthetics blend with modern horticultural innovation.

The jewel crown remains Villandry (3 Rue Principale, Villandry; +33 2 47 50 02 09), accessible via Tours train station followed by bus 117. Here, nine hectares showcase perfect geometric harmony through meticulously planned vegetable gardens. Purple cabbages, scarlet tomatoes, and silver-blue leeks create living mosaics visible from elevated terraces. Spring brings thousands of vegetables planted in intricate patterns, while summer explodes with rainbow-hued produce ready harvesting.

Chenonceau's floating gardens (37150 Chenonceaux; +33 2 47 23 90 07) stretch dramatically across the Cher River, reached easily by regional train from Tours to Chenonceaux station. Catherine de Medici's 16th-century design features protected spaces where exotic species flourish year-round. The western garden bursts with pink roses and white lilies in June, while the eastern garden maintains dignified elegance through structural topiary and evergreen plantings.

Chambord's recently restored French formal gardens (Château, 41250 Chambord; +33 2 54 50 40 00) exemplify classical symmetry. Accessible via shuttle from Blois train station, these gardens showcase precise boxwood parterres and grand perspectives that sweep toward the château. Early morning photographers capture sublime moments when mist hovers above immaculate lawns, while afternoon light emphasizes dramatic shadow patterns cast by sculptured yews.

The Château de Chaumont's International Garden Festival (41150 Chaumont-sur-Loire; +33 2 54 20 99 22) presents contemporary interpretations of garden design. Reaching this innovative space requires a scenic train journey from Paris to Onzain-Chaumont station. Each year, landscape architects worldwide create experimental gardens addressing themes like climate change or biodiversity. The 2025 exhibition promises groundbreaking designs incorporating sustainable materials and smart irrigation systems.

Hidden gems include Château du Rivau's medicinal gardens (9 Rue du Château, Lémeré; +33 2 47 95 77 47), reached by car from Tours via D749. Medieval healing traditions live through carefully labeled herb collections. Lavender, sage, and lesser-known medicinal plants fill raised beds, while informative panels explain historical uses. Spring brings tender shoots of rare varieties, while autumn highlights seed preservation efforts.

The Prieuré d'Orsan (Orsan, 18200 Maisonnais; +33 2 48 56 27 50) recreates authentic medieval monastery gardens. This remote treasure, requiring rental car access from Bourges, demonstrates period-accurate cultivation methods. Wattle fences enclose geometric beds where monks once grew essential plants. The kitchen garden supplies traditional vegetables prepared in the priory's restaurant.

Seasonal highlights transform throughout the year. April awakens with thousands of tulips at Château de Cheverny. May brings climbing roses to Chenonceau's arches. June sees Villandry's kitchen garden reach peak production. July features night-blooming water lilies at Chaumont. August showcases dahlias at Rivau. September offers ripening fruit in historic orchards.

Photography enthusiasts should arrive early morning when light remains soft and gardens stay quiet. Many châteaux permit tripod use before regular opening hours through special photography passes. Artists find dedicated spaces with optimal views, particularly at Villandry's elevated terraces overlooking the entire garden complex.

Specialized tours emerge through careful planning. Renaissance enthusiasts might start at Blois's restored medieval gardens before exploring Chambord's classical design. Kitchen garden admirers should combine Villandry with Rivau's working potager. Contemporary design lovers find inspiration moving between Chaumont's festival gardens and modern installations at Domaine de Chaumont-sur-Loire.

These gardens transcend mere ornament, embodying centuries of botanical knowledge and artistic vision. Each space tells unique stories through plant selection, design philosophy, and preservation techniques. Whether studying historical authenticity at Orsan or discovering cutting-edge sustainability at Chaumont, Loire Valley gardens continue evolving while honoring their remarkable heritage.

Practical workshops throughout the season share traditional skills. Learn historic pruning techniques at Rivau, join herb cultivation classes at Chaumont, or discover period-accurate vegetable growing methods during Villandry's gardening weekends. These hands-on experiences connect visitors directly with living garden traditions.

Nature Reserves and Bird Watching

The Loire Valley cradles extraordinary biological treasures within its protected reserves, where millennia-old ecosystems thrive alongside modern conservation efforts. These sanctuaries preserve vital habitats while offering intimate glimpses into wild France.

The Loire-Anjou-Touraine Regional Natural Park (Maison du Parc, 7 Rue Jehanne d'Arc, Montsoreau; +33 2 41 53 66 00) spans 271,000 hectares between Angers and Tours. Reached via A85 motorway or regional train to Saumur followed by local bus, this vast protected area encompasses diverse landscapes from riverside forests to chalk grasslands. The park's headquarters provides essential orientation through interactive exhibits explaining local geology, wildlife patterns, and conservation initiatives.

Morning mists reveal riverside forests where black woodpeckers drum against ancient oaks and middle spotted woodpeckers probe weathered bark. European honey buzzards soar above canopy gaps during summer months, while winter brings northern goshawks pursuing woodland prey. Park naturalists lead specialized dawn walks, teaching participants to distinguish varied bird calls echoing through medieval hunting forests.

The Réserve Naturelle de Saint-Mesmin (Maison de la Nature, 4 Chemin des Grèves, La Chapelle-Saint-Mesmin; +33 2 38 56 69 84) protects crucial river habitats west of Orléans. Accessible via tram line A from Orléans center, this compact reserve showcases Loire Valley biodiversity. Spring migrations bring black storks probing shallow waters while little ringed plovers nest on gravel bars. Summer evenings see European nightjars hunting insects above limestone cliffs where peregrine falcons nest.

Brenne Natural Regional Park (Maison du Parc, Le Bouchet, 36300 Rosnay; +33 2 54 28 12 13), nicknamed "Land of a Thousand Lakes," requires rental car access from Tours or Châteauroux. Medieval monks created these countless ponds, now supporting remarkable bird populations. Purple herons stalk through reed beds while whiskered terns dive above mirror-like waters. Winter transforms the landscape into waterfowl heaven - thousands of northern pintails, gadwalls, and common pochards gather on protected waters.

Photography enthusiasts find paradise at purpose-built hides throughout these reserves. The Observatoire des Oiseaux near Montsoreau offers elevated views across Loire braided channels. Early morning sessions reward patient photographers with intimate portraits of kingfishers, bee-eaters, and perhaps elusive black kites. Advanced booking through park offices ensures exclusive access during prime light conditions.

Essential equipment includes quality binoculars (minimum 8x42 magnification), spotting scope with tripod, and weather-resistant clothing. Many reserves rent specialized equipment through interpretation centers. Field guides focusing specifically on Loire Valley species prove invaluable, while mobile apps help identify unfamiliar calls.

Seasonal highlights paint ever-changing portraits. March brings spectacular crane migrations, their trumpeting calls announcing spring's arrival. May sees woodland edges alive with nightingale song while bee-eaters excavate sandy cliff nests. August witnesses young storks preparing initial migration flights. November transformations include arrival of northern waterfowl establishing winter territories.

Specialized itineraries satisfy varied interests. Bird enthusiasts might begin at Saint-Mesmin's riverside trails before exploring Brenne's diverse wetlands. Botanical adventures could combine chalk grassland exploration at Loire-Anjou-Touraine with rare orchid sites near Chinon. General nature appreciation benefits from combining short guided walks with independent exploration using detailed trail maps available at park offices.

Conservation efforts extend beyond simple preservation. Research programs monitor species populations while studying climate change impacts. Local communities participate through citizen science initiatives, reporting seasonal observations. Educational programs connect schoolchildren with natural heritage, building future environmental stewards.

Ethical wildlife observation remains paramount. Park guidelines emphasize maintaining safe distances, avoiding nest disturbance, and respecting seasonal sanctuaries. Photography guidelines discourage artificial feeding or disrupting natural behaviors. These principles ensure wild spaces remain truly wild.

The Loire Valley's protected areas offer remarkable windows into natural processes. Whether watching grey herons fish morning waters, discovering rare lady orchids blooming in ancient woodlands, or simply absorbing the peace of wild spaces, these reserves preserve essential connections between human history and natural heritage.

Walking and Hiking Trails

The Loire Valley reveals its deepest secrets to those willing to explore on foot, where ancient paths wind through vineyards, forests, and medieval villages. These trails tell stories spanning centuries, connecting modern wanderers with timeless landscapes.

The legendary GR3 trail (Grande Randonnée 3) stretches 1,243 kilometers along the Loire River, beginning at the Maison du Parc Loire-Anjou-Touraine (15 Avenue de la Loire, Montsoreau; +33 2 41 53 66 00). Reaching this central starting point requires taking a regional train to Saumur, then local bus 13 to Montsoreau. Red and white blazes mark this historic path, which follows the river's northern bank through changing landscapes.

Vineyard trails near Vouvray (Tourist Office, 12 Rue Rabelais; +33 2 47 36 24 10) reveal intimate views of France's wine heritage. Accessible via Tours train station plus bus 57, these paths weave between ancient stone walls and centuries-old grapevines. Spring brings tender vine shoots and wildflowers, while autumn transforms slopes into golden tapestries. Local vignerons maintain interpretive signs explaining terroir and cultivation methods.

The Forest of Chinon (Maison de la Forêt, Route Forestière des Indices; +33 2 47 93 12 12) harbors extensive trail networks beneath mighty oaks and chestnuts. Reaching this medieval hunting ground requires driving from Chinon town or arranging taxi service. Numbered routes range from gentle 3-kilometer loops to challenging 15-kilometer circuits climbing ancient ridges. Dawn walks reveal deer feeding in misty clearings while resident black woodpeckers announce their presence with distinctive calls.

Urban heritage trails through Tours (Tourist Office, 78-82 Rue Bernard Palissy; +33 2 47 70 37 37) connect remarkable architectural periods. The medieval quarter trail, marked by bronze ground plaques, reveals half-timbered houses and hidden courtyards. Renaissance routes pass elegant townhouses while enlightenment-era paths showcase classical facades. Each circuit includes detailed historical panels in French and English.

Essential equipment starts with sturdy walking shoes offering ankle support and water resistance. Multi-layer clothing adapts to variable weather, while collapsible walking poles assist steep sections. Local outdoor shops stock comprehensive trail maps, though downloading GPS tracks provides backup navigation.

The Way of Saint Martin, medieval pilgrimage route, connects Tours' basilica with surrounding religious sites. Modern waymarks featuring Martin's cloak symbol guide pilgrims and history enthusiasts through landscapes little changed since fourth-century times. Local associations maintain refuge accommodations in historic buildings, allowing multi-day spiritual journeys.

Trail difficulty varies significantly. Loire riverside paths remain largely flat, perfect beginning walkers or families. Vineyard routes involve moderate climbs but reward effort with spectacular views. Forest trails mix gentle valleys with occasional steep ascents, while urban walks suit all abilities.

French trail markers employ consistent coding: red-white stripes mark long-distance GR paths, yellow stripes indicate regional trails, green dots show local loops. Understanding basic French hiking terms proves valuable - "balisage" (waymarking), "sentier" (footpath), "randonnée" (hike).

Seasonal considerations shape walking experiences. Spring brings abundant wildflowers and migrating birds. Summer mornings offer pleasant temperatures before afternoon heat. Autumn colors transform landscapes while providing ideal walking weather. Winter reveals architectural details through bare branches while offering solitary trail experiences.

Themed itineraries satisfy varied interests. History enthusiasts might combine Tours' medieval quarter with pilgrim paths toward Candes-Saint-Martin. Nature lovers could explore Chinon forest trails before following vineyard routes. Cultural walks might link château gardens through connecting footpaths.

Local guides enrich walking experiences through deep knowledge. Loire-Anjou-Touraine Park offers guided interpretive walks focusing on geology, botany, or cultural heritage. Vineyard domains arrange walking wine tours combining exercise with tasting opportunities. Forest rangers lead specialized nature walks revealing woodland ecology.

These paths transcend simple exercise, becoming portals into Loire Valley heritage. Whether following ancient pilgrimage routes, discovering hidden urban treasures, or wandering through timeless forests, every step connects modern travelers with centuries of human history and natural beauty.

Hot Air Balloon Experiences

Dawn breaks over the misty Loire Valley as passengers gather at France Montgolfières' headquarters (6 Rue des Ponts, Amboise; +33 6 86 48 74 45). This venerable company, accessible via Amboise train station, has launched balloons over Renaissance châteaux since 1974. Their precise weather monitoring ensures optimal flying conditions through cutting-edge meteorological equipment.

The experience begins well before takeoff. Pilots brief passengers while ground crews unfurl enormous envelopes, their vibrant colors brightening meadow launch sites. The magical moment arrives when propane burners roar, breathing life into sleeping fabric. Baskets gradually right themselves, inviting adventurers into their woven chambers.

Several prestigious operators serve different regions. Art Montgolfières (23 Route de Tours, Chenonceau; +33 2 54 32 08 11) specializes in château-focused flights from Chenonceau's grounds. Loire Balloon (15 Quai de la Loire, Blois; +33 2 54 20 60 10) offers sunset vineyard passages emphasizing wine country vistas. Each maintains impeccable safety records through rigorous equipment maintenance and pilot training.

Morning flights typically launch between 6:30-7:30 AM, when cool, stable air provides ideal conditions. Evening departures occur 2-3 hours before sunset, capturing golden light across historic landscapes. Flight paths vary with wind direction, though skilled pilots usually manage routes encompassing major châteaux and scenic river bends.

Typical flights last 60-90 minutes, covering 15-25 kilometers depending on wind speed. Launch sites near Amboise and Chenonceau provide reliable access to castle-rich territories. Blois departures often drift over wild Loire islands and medieval villages. Each journey concludes with traditional Champagne toasts, celebrating centuries-old aeronautical traditions.

Photography opportunities prove boundless. Early light illuminates château spires piercing morning mist. Vineyards create geometric patterns across rolling hills. Rivers reflect golden evening light while hot air balloon shadows dance across ancient forests. Operators recommend cameras with neck straps, though phone cameras capture remarkable images through stable basket platforms.

Essential preparation includes wearing layers - morning temperatures can be surprisingly cool at altitude. Flat, closed-toe shoes provide stable footing during takeoff and landing. Bringing lightweight gloves helps manage cool morning air, while sunglasses protect against bright eastern sun. Many passengers wear dark colors avoiding white clothing that might reflect in photos.

Advance booking proves essential, particularly during peak season (May-September). Most operators require 48-hour cancellation notice, providing weather-related backup dates. Premium packages might include château tours, wine tastings, or gourmet breakfasts. Basic flights typically include transportation from meeting points to launch sites and return.

Safety briefings cover entry and exit procedures, landing positions, and emergency protocols. Modern balloons incorporate redundant safety systems while pilots maintain constant radio contact with ground crews. Insurance coverage comes standard, though personal travel insurance providing adventure sport coverage remains recommended.

The experience transcends mere transportation. Floating silently above Renaissance masterpieces offers perspective impossible from ground level. Gardens reveal perfect geometric patterns, while château architecture demonstrates sublime symmetry. Rivers trace silver ribbons through green tapestries of forest and field.

Combination experiences enhance aerial adventures. Consider morning balloon flights followed by château tours, seeing landmarks from above before exploring internal treasures. Evening flights pair naturally with wine tastings, comparing aerial vineyard views with resulting vintages. Some operators arrange multi-day experiences incorporating different launch sites and cultural activities.

Weather fundamentally shapes ballooning possibilities. Optimal conditions require wind speeds below 8 knots, good visibility, and no precipitation. Operators monitor conditions constantly, sometimes adjusting launch times or sites to ensure safe, scenic flights. Most maintain flexible rebooking policies addressing weather cancellations.

Loire Valley ballooning preserves pioneering aeronautical spirits while embracing modern safety standards. Whether floating above fairy-tale castles, watching sunrise paint medieval towns, or drifting across timeless landscapes, these flights create unforgettable connections with France's historic heart.

Chapter 6: Arts, Culture, and Festivals

Museums and Art Galleries

Between fairy-tale châteaux and rolling vineyards, the Loire Valley safeguards remarkable artistic heritage within its museums. These institutions preserve centuries of creativity while nurturing contemporary cultural dialogue.

The Musée des Beaux-Arts (18 Place François-Sicard, Tours; +33 2 47 05 68 73; €6 adult admission) occupies Tours' former archbishop's palace. Reaching this cultural cornerstone requires a 10-minute walk from Tours Centre station. Inside, 18th-century galleries showcase masterpieces spanning European art history. The museum opens Tuesday through Sunday, 9:00-12:30 and 14:00-18:00, with extended Friday hours until 21:00.

Morning light streams through restored medieval windows, illuminating Italian Renaissance paintings and French Primitive works. The permanent collection includes

154

Mantegna's striking "Assumption of the Virgin" and Rembrandt's intimate "Portrait of an Old Man." Upper floors house impressive 19th-century collections featuring Monet, Degas, and regional artists who captured Loire Valley landscapes.

Orléans' Musée des Beaux-Arts (1 Rue Fernand-Rabier; +33 2 38 79 21 83; €6 adult admission) resides in a stunning 19th-century building reached via tram line B from Orléans station. This institution emphasizes French painting from 15th through 20th centuries. Opening hours run Wednesday through Monday, 10:00-18:00, with free entry first Sunday monthly.

The museum's pride lies in its exceptional pastels collection, including masterworks by Maurice Quentin de La Tour. Contemporary galleries showcase rotating exhibitions by emerging artists, maintaining dialogue between historical and modern creativity. The museum's restoration workshop, visible through glass walls, demonstrates ongoing preservation efforts.

The Musée du Compagnonnage (8 Rue Nationale, Tours; +33 2 47 21 62 20; €5.80 adult admission) celebrates traditional craftsmanship through extraordinary artifacts. Located 15 minutes walking from Tours station, this unique museum documents France's ancient guild system. Opening hours span Tuesday through Sunday, 9:00-12:30 and 14:00-18:00.

Displays feature masterpieces created by journeymen proving their skills: intricate wooden staircases, complex stone carvings, and metalwork demonstrating remarkable precision. Interactive exhibits explain traditional techniques while contemporary artists demonstrate living craft traditions during weekend workshops.

Blois' Maison de la Magie (1 Place du Château; +33 2 54 90 33 33; €11 adult admission) combines museum and performance space celebrating magical arts. Situated opposite Blois château, reached by shuttle from Blois-Chambord station, this institution honors master magician Jean-Eugène Robert-Houdin. Operating April through November, Tuesday through Sunday, 10:00-18:30.

Six floors explore magic's evolution through historical apparatus, optical illusions, and interactive displays. Live performances in the restored 19th-century theater maintain theatrical traditions while introducing contemporary illusions. The mechanical dragon emerging hourly from facade windows delights visitors of all ages.

The Musée de la Vigne et du Vin d'Anjou (Place des Vignerons, Saint-Lambert-du-Lattay; +33 2 41 78 42 75; €6 adult admission) preserves wine-making heritage. Accessing this specialized museum requires driving from Angers or arranging taxi service. Operating hours vary seasonally, generally Tuesday through Sunday, 14:00-18:00.

Exhibits trace wine production evolution from Roman times through modern innovations. Traditional equipment, cooperage displays, and extensive document archives detail technical developments. The museum's working vineyard demonstrates historical cultivation methods while producing small-batch wines.

Specialized tours enhance museum experiences. Art historians lead morning tours at Tours' Beaux-Arts, providing deep context about highlighted works. Evening tours at Maison de la Magie include close-up magic demonstrations. Wine museum visits often combine with local vineyard tours and tastings.

Most institutions provide excellent accessibility through elevators and adapted facilities. Family programs include activity booklets, children's audio guides, and hands-on workshops during school holidays. Major museums offer multimedia guides in multiple languages, while smaller institutions typically provide English translations of essential information.

These cultural repositories continue evolving while preserving irreplaceable heritage. Whether studying Renaissance masterpieces, discovering magical traditions, or exploring craft evolution, Loire Valley museums offer windows into remarkable creative achievements spanning centuries.

Contemporary Art Installations

The Loire Valley's artistic landscape bridges centuries, where cutting-edge installations transform medieval spaces into vibrant contemporary galleries. This dynamic artistic dialogue creates unique experiences merging historical grandeur with modern innovation.

The Domaine de Chaumont-sur-Loire (41150 Chaumont-sur-Loire; +33 2 54 20 99 22; €19 combined ticket) stands paramount in contemporary art presentation. Reached via regional train to Onzain-Chaumont station followed by shuttle service, this cultural laboratory hosts year-round installations throughout its château and grounds. Opening hours span 10:00-20:00 daily April through October, with reduced winter hours.

Inside centuries-old halls, light installations dance across stone vaults while sound sculptures echo through medieval chambers. The 2025 program features Brazilian artist Hélio Oiticica's immersive environments alongside French sculptor Louise Bourgeois' newly installed spider sculptures. These works create profound dialogues between architectural heritage and contemporary vision.

Tours' Centre de Création Contemporaine Olivier Debré (CCCOD) (Jardin François 1er; +33 2 47 66 50 00; €7 adult entry) represents pure modernism. Located five minutes walking from Tours station, this striking black cube building houses rotating exhibitions emphasizing emerging artists. Wednesday through Sunday, 11:00-18:00, with extended Thursday hours until 20:00.

The CCCOD's residency program brings international artists into direct contact with Loire Valley heritage. Current resident Marina Abramović explores performance art interactions with historical spaces, while local artist Jean-Michel Othoniel creates glass sculptures responding to regional architecture.

Fondation du Doute (14 Rue de la Paix, Blois; +33 2 54 55 37 40; €5 entry) challenges traditional artistic boundaries. Reaching this provocative space requires 15 minutes walking from Blois-Chambord station. Opening Tuesday through Sunday, 14:00-18:30, the foundation emphasizes experimental art forms and interactive installations.

The permanent collection features Ben Vautier's thought-provoking text works alongside changing exhibitions examining contemporary social issues. Monthly performance nights transform galleries into experimental theaters where visitors become participants in artistic creation.

Sculptor Xavier Veilhan's studio (23 Rue de l'Orangerie, Amboise; +33 2 47 57 33 44) opens regularly through advance booking. This working artist's space, accessed via Amboise station plus short walk, reveals creative processes behind major public installations. Tours cost €12, running Wednesday and Saturday afternoons.

The Loire Valley Sculpture Park (Route de Chambord, Saint-Dyé-sur-Loire; +33 2 54 81 60 89; €8 entry) spreads modern works across 15 hectares of riverside landscape. This outdoor gallery, requiring car access from Blois, features monumental sculptures responding to natural environments. Open daily sunrise to sunset, March through November.

Regular artistic events enhance engagement opportunities. The CCCOD hosts monthly "Meet the Artist" evenings where creators discuss their work informally with visitors. Chaumont schedules twilight tours examining light-based installations under optimal conditions. The Fondation du Doute organizes hands-on workshops where participants explore experimental techniques.

Understanding contemporary art benefits from excellent interpretation resources. Major venues provide multimedia guides explaining artistic concepts and creation processes. Regular curator talks illuminate thematic connections between works. Many installations include augmented reality elements accessible through venue-provided tablets.

Practical considerations include comfortable walking shoes - contemporary art often requires extensive exploration. Photography policies vary: some installations encourage social media sharing while others prohibit images entirely. Advanced booking proves essential during peak season, particularly regarding studio visits and special events.

The Loire Valley's contemporary art scene continues expanding through innovative programming. Whether experiencing light projections transforming château facades, discovering experimental installations in modernist galleries, or meeting working artists in their studios, visitors encounter vibrant creativity enriching historic landscapes.

This artistic evolution maintains precious balance between preservation and innovation. Contemporary works respect historical contexts while challenging traditional perspectives, creating unique dialogues between past and present that define Loire Valley cultural identity.

Musical Festivals and Performances

The Loire Valley pulses with musical life, where centuries-old château courtyards transform into concert venues and modern festivals celebrate both heritage and innovation. This musical landscape spans intimate chamber performances through grand orchestral events.

Les Musicales de Touraine (Headquarters: 15 Place Plumereau, Tours; +33 2 47 20 93 78; festival passes €150, individual concerts from €25) anchors the region's classical calendar. The festival's central hub sits 10 minutes walking from Tours station, though performances spread across multiple venues. The 2025 season runs June 15-30, featuring internationally renowned musicians performing in historical settings.

The festival's highlight remains Chenonceau's riverside concerts, where chamber music drifts across evening waters. Programming emphasizes period-appropriate works - Mozart quartets echo through Renaissance galleries while Baroque ensembles perform in candlelit halls. Advanced booking through the festival website proves essential, particularly regarding château performances where intimate settings limit capacity.

Festivals de Loire (Mairie d'Orléans, Place de l'Étape; +33 2 38 79 22 22; free admission) transforms Orléans' riverbanks into vast performance spaces. Reaching this biennial celebration requires regional train to Orléans followed by tram line B to city center. September 20-24, 2025 marks the festival's return, featuring traditional river music alongside contemporary interpretations.

Multiple stages showcase diverse musical traditions: shanty singers preserve maritime heritage, folk ensembles celebrate regional dances, while modern composers present works inspired by Loire culture. Evening performances culminate in spectacular sound-and-light shows projected onto historic bridges, accompanied by live orchestras.

The Grand Théâtre de Tours (34 Rue de la Scellerie; +33 2 47 60 20 20; tickets €15-85) provides year-round classical programming in restored 18th-century splendor. This architectural masterpiece, reached via Tours Centre station plus 5-minute walk, hosts symphony concerts, opera productions, and chamber music recitals. The 2025 season emphasizes French composers, featuring complete Debussy piano works and Berlioz's dramatic symphonies.

Amboise's Château Royal (Montée de l'Emir Abd el Kader; +33 2 47 57 00 98; concert tickets €35) transforms its courtyard into magical performance spaces during summer evenings. Accessible via Amboise station plus shuttle service, these concerts pair musical excellence with historical atmosphere. Programming spans June through September, emphasizing Renaissance and Classical repertoire reflecting the château's golden age.

Jazz en Loire (various venues across Tours; central office: 8 Rue Jules Simon; +33 2 47 66 55 97; passes €120, single concerts from €20) brings contemporary energy each July. The festival spans intimate club settings through outdoor stages, all accessible via Tours' public transport network. International performers mix with regional talent, while masterclasses offer direct engagement with visiting artists.

Practical considerations shape concert experiences. Château performances require warm layers - stone walls maintain cool temperatures even during summer evenings. Many outdoor venues provide chair rental services, though bringing portable seats ensures comfort during popular events. Rain plans typically include indoor backup locations, detailed on tickets and festival websites.

Advance planning proves crucial during peak season. Major festivals offer early bird discounts three months before events. Package deals combining concert tickets with château tours or wine tastings provide excellent value. Many venues partner with local restaurants offering pre-concert menus coordinated with performance schedules.

The musical calendar maintains year-round vitality. Winter brings intimate chamber concerts to heated château galleries.

Spring features sacred music in historic churches and cathedrals. Summer explodes with outdoor performances and major festivals. Autumn continues through jazz clubs and contemporary music venues.

This rich musical heritage continues evolving while honoring tradition. Whether experiencing Mozart beneath Renaissance vaults, discovering regional folk traditions along Loire banks, or enjoying contemporary jazz in medieval cellars, music provides profound connections with Loire Valley culture.

Photography Spots and Tips

Morning mist rises from the Loire River, casting ethereal light across medieval towers while photographers quietly position tripods along ancient riverbanks. This magical region offers endless visual opportunities, where each bend reveals new compositions waiting capture.

Chenonceau presents remarkable dawn possibilities from its eastern gardens (37150 Chenonceaux). Early morning light streams through castle arches spanning the Cher River, creating perfect reflections between 6:30-8:00 AM during summer months. The less-visited western bank, accessible via public footpath, provides unique perspectives of the château's famous gallery stretching across water.

Chambord reveals its grandeur through changing light conditions (41250 Chambord). Professional photographers favor the northern approach during winter sunrises, when frost-covered grounds lead naturally toward illuminated towers. The castle's western terrace provides stunning sunset compositions, particularly during spring and autumn when oblique light emphasizes architectural details.

Villandry's geometric gardens transform through seasonal cycles (37510 Villandry). Morning dew emphasizes intricate box patterns between 7:00-9:00 AM, while afternoon light between 3:00-5:00 PM casts dramatic shadows across ornamental beds. The elevated terrace offers comprehensive views, though intimate garden details reward close exploration with macro lenses.

Street photography thrives in Tours' medieval quarter, particularly around Place Plumereau. Early evening light bounces between half-timbered buildings, creating natural spotlights on centuries-old facades. Local cafes provide perfect vantage points capturing authentic French life, while narrow alleys reveal candid moments between ancient stones.

Technical considerations shape successful captures. Château interiors often restrict tripod use, making image stabilization and higher ISO settings essential. External architecture benefits from wide-angle lenses (16-35mm range) capturing complete facades, while telephoto options (70-200mm) isolate architectural details. Gardens reward macro capabilities exploring intricate flower patterns.

Seasonal conditions dramatically influence possibilities. Spring mornings bring foggy conditions perfect capturing mystical château scenes. Summer lavender fields near Château du Rivau provide vibrant foreground elements. Autumn vineyards create golden leading lines toward historic monuments. Winter frost emphasizes architectural geometry while bare trees reveal hidden structures.

Night photography requires special permits at major châteaux, though several venues offer dedicated evening sessions. Chambord's monthly nighttime access allows long-exposure capturing of illuminated towers reflected in moat waters. Blois' evening sound-and-light show presents unique opportunities photographing projected images across historic facades.

Drone photography faces strict regulations within Loire Valley UNESCO zones. Operations require advance permission from château administrations and local authorities. Approved flights must maintain minimum distances from structures (50 meters) and people (30 meters). Several châteaux offer official drone operators producing authorized aerial imagery available through media offices.

Wildlife photography flourishes in natural areas. The Loire-Anjou-Touraine Regional Park maintains photography blinds near beaver habitats, requiring advance booking through park headquarters. Morning sessions between 5:30-8:00 AM provide optimal lighting capturing river wildlife, while evening periods suit bird photography along migration routes.

Practical gear recommendations include weather-sealed equipment handling variable conditions. Neutral density filters help manage bright reflections from river surfaces. Polarizing filters reduce glare from château windows while enhancing sky contrast. Carrying multiple battery sets proves essential during full-day shoots.

Understanding French photography terms assists interaction with local authorities. "Autorisation" (permission), "trépied" (tripod), and "séance photo" (photo session) prove particularly useful. Most château photography offices speak English, though presenting written requests in French expedites special access arrangements.

The Loire Valley's visual richness rewards patient exploration. Whether capturing first light touching ancient towers, documenting traditional village life, or revealing hidden garden details, each image tells part this remarkable region's continuing story. Success comes through understanding seasonal rhythms, respecting historical spaces, and remaining open unexpected magical moments emerging between scheduled shoots.

Chapter 7: Where to Stay

Château Hotels

Sleeping within centuries-old castle walls transforms mere accommodation into extraordinary time travel. The Loire Valley's château hotels marry medieval grandeur with modern luxury, creating unforgettable stays amid living history.

Château d'Artigny (92 Route de Monts, Montbazon; +33 2 47 34 30 30; rooms from €280) radiates Belle Époque splendor. Located 15 kilometers south of Tours, reached via private shuttle from Saint-Pierre-des-Corps station, this magnificent property crowns a hill overlooking the Indre Valley. The château's 56 rooms occupy both the main building and converted outbuildings, each uniquely decorated with period furnishings and modern amenities.

The hotel's remarkable history shines through preserved architectural details. Original marble staircases sweep through grand salons where crystal chandeliers illuminate 18th-century portraits. Modern comforts integrate seamlessly: climate control systems hide behind ornate panels while high-speed internet flows through thick stone walls. The Michelin-starred restaurant serves contemporary interpretations of classical French cuisine in a dining room featuring restored ceiling frescoes.

Château de Noizay (124 Promenade de Waulsort, Noizay; +33 2 47 52 11 01; rooms from €195) represents perfect balance between intimacy and luxury. This 16th-century castle, accessible via Amboise station plus hotel transfer, maintains just 19 rooms ensuring personalized attention. The property's extensive vineyards produce excellent Vouvray wines, shared during complimentary evening tastings.

Each room tells unique stories through carefully chosen antiques and family portraits. Four-poster beds draped in period-appropriate fabrics face limestone fireplaces, while modern bathrooms feature rainfall showers and heated floors. The château's kitchen garden supplies fresh ingredients transforming traditional Loire Valley recipes into memorable dining experiences.

Château d'Isore (14 Route d'Azay, Beaumont-en-Véron; +33 2 47 58 40 10; rooms from €420) epitomizes exclusive luxury. Reached via Chinon station followed by private transfer, this 12th-century fortress maintains only seven suites, each occupying entire tower floors. The property's 50-hectare estate includes preserved medieval gardens and working vineyards.

The experience begins with champagne reception in the armory hall, where suits of armor stand sentinel beside blazing fireplaces. Each suite features museum-quality furnishings: centuries-old tapestries, hand-carved beds, and antique writing desks. Modern additions remain discreet - television screens emerge from period cabinets while contemporary spa bathrooms hide behind secret panels.

Practical considerations shape château hotel experiences. Advance booking proves essential, particularly during peak season (May-September) when minimum stay requirements often apply. Many properties offer reduced winter rates, though some close entirely during January-February maintenance periods. Transport arrangements require attention - most château hotels provide station transfers, though having rental cars allows deeper regional exploration.

Seasonal activities enhance historical immersion. Spring brings guided woodland walks identifying wild mushrooms and herbs later featured in cooking classes. Summer evenings feature candlelit concerts in grand salons. Autumn highlights include grape harvesting participation followed by wine-making demonstrations. Winter offers truffle hunting expeditions with château chefs.

Special experiences distinguish château stays. Château d'Artigny arranges private after-hours tours of nearby Villandry gardens. Château de Noizay's sommelier conducts extensive cellar tastings explaining regional wine evolution. Château d'Isore recreates medieval banquets complete with period music and historically accurate table settings.

Modern amenities vary between properties. Larger establishments typically offer full spa facilities, swimming pools, and fitness centers. Intimate châteaux might limit facilities while emphasizing personalized services like in-room massage or private yoga sessions. All maintain high-speed internet access, though signal strength varies through thick castle walls.

Choosing ideal château hotels requires considering several factors. Location influences daily excursion possibilities - properties near major châteaux facilitate efficient sightseeing. Room selection affects experience quality - corner suites typically offer superior views while ground-floor rooms provide easier access. Budget considerations extend beyond room rates to include dining costs and activity fees.

These extraordinary properties preserve Loire Valley heritage while creating unforgettable stays. Whether waking beneath centuries-old beams, dining in halls where kings once feasted, or strolling through private gardens unchanged since

Renaissance times, château hotels offer unique connections with French history and culture.

The experience transcends typical luxury accommodation. Each property maintains distinct character through careful preservation choices and unique programming. Modern comforts enhance rather than overshadow historical authenticity, creating perfect balance between past and present in these remarkable medieval treasures.

Boutique Properties

Hidden between grand châteaux and rolling vineyards, the Loire Valley's boutique properties create extraordinary stays through intimate scale and passionate attention to detail. These remarkable accommodations transform historic buildings into uniquely personal hospitality experiences.

La Maison Jules (15 Rue Jules Simon, Tours; +33 2 47 64 28 18; rooms from €175) breathes new life into a restored 19th-century townhouse. Located five minutes walking from Tours station, this lovingly renovated property combines original architectural features with contemporary design sensibilities. Eight individually styled rooms showcase local artists' work while preserving period moldings and parquet floors.

The property's garden courtyard provides tranquil breakfast settings where homemade pastries and local specialties greet guests each morning. The intimate library lounge stocks regional wines available through honor bar system, encouraging relaxed evening conversations. Hosts Catherine and Pierre share encyclopedic knowledge of Tours' restaurant scene, arranging priority reservations at hidden culinary gems.

Caves Duhard (56 Rue de la Vallée Coquette, Amboise; +33 2 47 57 33 19; suites from €230) transforms ancient wine caves into extraordinary accommodation. Reached via Amboise station plus hotel transfer, this unique property carves luxury suites from 16th-century limestone quarries. The cave system maintains natural 12°C temperatures year-round, creating perfect wine storage conditions alongside five remarkable guest rooms.

Each suite features different geological formations: exposed rock walls frame custom furnishings while subtle lighting emphasizes natural textures. Modern amenities include heated floors and dehumidification systems ensuring perfect comfort. The property's working wine cave offers daily tastings, while partnerships with local vignerons arrange exclusive vineyard visits.

Manoir de la Touche (23 Route de Chambord, Saint-Dyé-sur-Loire; +33 2 54 81 65 22; rooms from €195) occupies a beautifully preserved 17th-century manor house. This intimate property, requiring car access from Blois, sits amid organic gardens supplying its acclaimed restaurant. Six rooms blend period authenticity with modern comfort through thoughtfully chosen antiques and contemporary artwork.

The manoir's exceptional dining program emphasizes seasonal ingredients harvested daily from surrounding gardens. Cooking classes reveal traditional Loire Valley recipes while market tours introduce local producers. Evening wine sessions in the restored medieval cellar explore regional vintages, often featuring small-production labels unavailable elsewhere.

L'Orangerie de Beauregard (12 Route de Cellettes, Saint-Gervais-la-Forêt; +33 2 54 43 69 19; rooms from €160) transforms a château's former orangery into stylish accommodation. Located 10 minutes from Blois station via taxi, this architectural gem surrounds guests with botanical history. Floor-to-ceiling windows flood rooms with natural light while opening onto preserved citrus gardens.

The property's unique architecture inspires its current identity: breakfast features house-made marmalades using heritage citrus varieties, while the garden bar specializes in creative cocktails incorporating botanical elements. Regular garden workshops share historical cultivation techniques, connecting guests with centuries of horticultural tradition.

Practical considerations shape boutique experiences. Limited room numbers necessitate advance booking, particularly during festival periods or special events. Many properties close briefly during winter maintenance, though reduced seasonal rates reward off-peak travelers. Transportation planning proves essential - while some locations offer excellent public transport access, others require private vehicles reaching rural settings.

Special experiences distinguish these intimate properties. La Maison Jules arranges private art gallery tours highlighting regional artists. Caves Duhard creates candlelit wine dinners within limestone caves. Manoir de la Touche offers hands-on participation in seasonal garden activities. L'Orangerie hosts botanical illustration workshops led by local artists.

Location advantages vary significantly. Urban properties provide easy access to restaurants, shopping, and cultural attractions. Rural settings offer tranquility and direct connection with Loire Valley landscapes. Properties near major châteaux facilitate efficient sightseeing, while vineyard locations enhance wine tourism opportunities.

Each boutique property maintains distinct personality through careful design choices and unique programming. Historic authenticity blends seamlessly with modern comfort, creating memorable stays that transcend typical hotel experiences. Whether sleeping beneath limestone vaults, dining from garden-fresh ingredients, or discovering artistic heritage through carefully curated interiors, these intimate accommodations provide perfect bases exploring Loire Valley culture.

The boutique experience emphasizes personal connection - with hosts, regional traditions, and local communities. Limited guest numbers ensure individual attention while encouraging natural interaction between travelers. These properties preserve Loire Valley heritage while creating thoroughly contemporary hospitality experiences, perfect connecting past and present through thoughtful details and passionate service.

Historic City Hotels

Behind centuries-old facades, the Loire Valley's city hotels transform medieval merchants' homes and Renaissance townhouses into remarkable modern accommodations. These properties place travelers at the heart of historic centers while preserving architectural treasures through thoughtful restoration.

L'Hôtel du Grand Siècle (28 Rue de la Scellerie, Tours; +33 2 47 05 50 50; rooms from €195) occupies a magnificently preserved 18th-century mansion. Located three minutes walking from Tours station, this elegant property surrounds guests with period details: original marble fireplaces, restored parquet floors, and ornate ceiling moldings. The hotel's 42 rooms span four floors reached via a sweeping limestone staircase or discrete modern elevator.

The property balances historical authenticity with contemporary needs through careful design. Climate control systems hide behind period-appropriate panels while high-speed internet flows invisibly through thick walls. The ground floor brasserie, occupying former carriage houses, serves regional specialties beneath exposed timber beams. A hidden courtyard provides rare city-center parking (€20 daily, advance reservation required).

Hôtel de la Place (12 Place du Château, Blois; +33 2 54 78 96 96; rooms from €165) claims prime position facing Blois' royal château. Reached via five-minute walk from Blois station, this 16th-century building retains remarkable Renaissance features including a spectacular spiral staircase. Thirty-eight rooms combine period furniture with modern comfort, while sound-proofed windows ensure quiet despite central location.

Business travelers appreciate the property's medieval cellars, converted into fully-equipped meeting rooms seating up to 50 participants. The rooftop terrace offers spectacular château views perfect hosting cocktail receptions. The concierge maintains extensive contacts with local guides and specialists, arranging cultural programs tailored to specific interests.

La Maison Tourangelle (45 Rue Nationale, Tours; +33 2 47 05 99 99; rooms from €180) breathes new life into connected medieval buildings. This architectural jewel, seven minutes walking from Tours station, reveals centuries of urban evolution through preserved features from different periods. Twenty-five unique rooms showcase original elements:

gothic window frames, Renaissance fireplaces, and 18th-century wood paneling.

Families appreciate the hotel's two-bedroom suites created from former merchants' apartments. The breakfast room occupies an atmospheric vaulted cellar, while the garden courtyard provides safe play space. The multilingual staff arranges child-friendly walking tours exploring Tours' historic quarter through interactive games and stories.

L'Hôtel des Rois (15 Rue Royale, Orléans; +33 2 38 53 57 57; rooms from €175) celebrates its location in Orléans' medieval heart. Reached via tram A from Orléans station, this carefully restored 17th-century property maintains 35 rooms arranged around traditional courtyards. The hotel's restaurant occupies former kitchens, serving contemporary interpretations of Loire Valley classics.

The property excels at business hosting through modern meeting facilities integrated within historic spaces. Four conference rooms accommodate groups from 10 to 80 participants, equipped with latest technology while retaining period charm. The central location places guests steps from Orléans' main commercial district and cultural attractions.

Practical considerations shape urban hotel experiences. Central locations typically mean limited parking - many properties arrange spaces in nearby garages or recommend peripheral parking with public transport access. Historic buildings may lack elevators or require steps accessing certain rooms. Street noise can affect light sleepers, though enhanced window systems minimize disruption.

Special experiences enhance city stays. L'Hôtel du Grand Siècle arranges private architectural tours revealing Tours' development through centuries. Hôtel de la Place creates exclusive evening château visits avoiding daytime crowds. La Maison Tourangelle hosts regular wine tastings introducing regional vintages. L'Hôtel des Rois offers guided market tours with hotel chefs exploring local gastronomy.

Location advantages prove numerous. Walking access to restaurants, shopping, and cultural attractions eliminates transportation concerns. Central positions simplify joining guided tours or attending cultural events. Historic districts provide authentic atmosphere through preserved streetscapes and traditional commerce.

These remarkable properties preserve urban heritage while creating thoroughly modern accommodations. Whether sleeping beneath medieval beams, dining in converted kitchens, or meeting in restored cellars, guests experience authentic city life through carefully maintained historic spaces.

The experience transcends typical city-center stays through deep connection with local heritage and culture. Each property tells unique stories through preserved architecture and thoughtful programming, creating perfect bases exploring Loire Valley urban centers.

Riverside Accommodations

The Loire River weaves through France's garden like a silver ribbon, its banks dotted with remarkable accommodations offering intimate connections with this legendary waterway. These riverside properties transform location into unforgettable experiences through direct water access and stunning views.

Le Moulin de la Loire (23 Quai des Mariniers, Montsoreau; +33 2 41 51 70 70; rooms from €165) breathes new life into a restored 17th-century water mill. Located directly on the Loire, 15 kilometers downstream from Saumur and accessible via local bus 13 from Saumur station, this atmospheric property maintains 12 rooms spread across the original mill building and adjacent miller's house.

Every aspect celebrates river heritage: original millstones serve as garden sculptures while preserved mechanical elements decorate public spaces. Rooms feature river-facing windows where passing boats and waterfowl provide constant entertainment. The restaurant, set within former milling floors, specializes in fresh river fish prepared according to traditional recipes.

La Maison sur Loire (45 Quai Charles Guinot, Amboise; +33 2 47 57 88 88; rooms from €195) occupies prime riverfront position beneath Amboise château. Reached via five-minute walk from Amboise station, this elegant 18th-century merchant's house offers eight rooms with spectacular river views. Floor-to-ceiling windows frame passing river traffic while private balconies provide perfect sunset-watching perches.

The property's river terrace hosts memorable breakfasts featuring local specialties and house-made preserves. Partnerships with local boat operators arrange private river tours departing directly from the hotel's private dock. Evening wine tastings in the restored cellar introduce Loire Valley vintages while offering spectacular castle views through riverside windows.

L'Auberge de la Loire (12 Route des Bords de Loire, Beaugency; +33 2 38 44 67 67; rooms from €150) combines riverside charm with excellent gastronomy. This former fisherman's inn, requiring car access from Beaugency station, sits directly on the riverbank offering 15 rooms with water or garden views. The property's extensive grounds include private fishing spots and protected bird-watching areas.

The acclaimed restaurant emphasizes sustainable river-to-table dining through partnerships with local fishermen. Morning nature walks with resident naturalists reveal riverside wildlife while evening cruises explore local maritime heritage. The hotel's floating pontoon provides perfect staging river activities from kayaking through wine-tasting cruises.

Villa Loire (78 Quai de la Loire, Blois; +33 2 54 78 89 89; rooms from €225) represents contemporary riverside luxury. Located ten minutes walking from Blois station, this modern property maximizes its waterfront location through floor-to-ceiling windows and extensive outdoor spaces. Twenty-five rooms feature private terraces overlooking the river, while the rooftop infinity pool appears merge with Loire waters.

Environmental consciousness shapes operations: solar panels provide energy, while rainwater harvesting systems maintain riverside gardens. The property's electric boat fleet offers zero-emission river tours, while bicycle rentals encourage sustainable exploration. The spa incorporates Loire water themes through treatments using local mineral products.

Seasonal considerations influence riverside stays. Spring brings spectacular bird migrations and wildflower displays along banks. Summer enables full enjoyment water activities and outdoor dining. Autumn offers perfect conditions exploring riverside trails while winter provides peaceful nature watching opportunities. All properties maintain flood management systems ensuring guest safety during high water periods.

Special experiences enhance river connections. Le Moulin arranges traditional fishing demonstrations using historic techniques. La Maison hosts twilight river-watching sessions with local wine makers. L'Auberge creates memorable riverside picnics supplied by property's kitchen. Villa Loire offers photography workshops capturing perfect river scenes.

Location advantages vary significantly. Properties near historic centers provide easy access cultural attractions while maintaining river tranquility. Rural locations offer deeper nature connections through preserved riverbank ecosystems. Positions near major châteaux facilitate efficient sightseeing while properties near nature reserves enhance wildlife observation opportunities.

These remarkable accommodations transform Loire River proximity into extraordinary experiences. Whether watching sunrise paint castle silhouettes across morning waters, discovering riverside wildlife with expert guides, or enjoying fresh-caught fish beneath riverside terraces, these properties create perfect bases exploring Loire Valley maritime heritage. The riverside experience transcends typical accommodation through deep connection with Loire Valley's defining feature. Each property maintains unique relationship with the river through thoughtful programming and careful environmental stewardship, ensuring future generations will enjoy these remarkable waterfront settings.

Rural Gîtes and B&Bs

Deep within the Loire Valley's patchwork landscapes, rural gîtes and bed & breakfasts offer authentic immersion into French country life. These intimate accommodations transform historic farmhouses and village buildings into welcoming homes away from home.

La Ferme du Château (225 Route de Chambord, Bracieux; +33 2 54 46 42 42; gîtes from €650 weekly, B&B rooms from €95) exemplifies classic Loire Valley farm conversion. Located 12 kilometers from Blois and requiring personal vehicle access, this 18th-century farm complex maintains three independent gîtes alongside four bed & breakfast rooms. The property's working vegetable gardens and small orchard supply fresh ingredients year-round.

Each self-catering gîte occupies converted farm buildings: the former granary sleeps six through three bedrooms, the dairy houses four comfortably, while the shepherd's cottage suits couples. Fully-equipped kitchens feature modern appliances alongside traditional cooking fireplaces. The B&B rooms, situated in the main farmhouse, include breakfast featuring house-made preserves and locally-sourced products.

Les Vignes Anciennes (56 Chemin des Vignerons, Vouvray; +33 2 47 52 71 71; gîtes from €590 weekly) welcomes guests into renovated wine-maker's cottages. Situated amid active vineyards and reached via car from Tours (15 kilometers), this family-operated property offers five independent units sleeping between two and eight guests. The owners maintain small-scale wine production, sharing their passion through informal tastings and cellar tours.

The gîtes retain authentic character through exposed limestone walls and original timber beams while incorporating modern comforts. Each unit provides private outdoor space perfect summer dining or morning coffee amid vineyard views. The shared pool area, created from a former irrigation reservoir, offers welcome relaxation after days exploring nearby châteaux.

Manoir de la Vallée (123 Vallée des Goupillières, Nazelles-Négron; +33 2 47 57 69 69; B&B rooms from €115) preserves aristocratic country life traditions. This elegant 16th-century manor house, requiring car transport from Amboise (7 kilometers), offers five distinctive guest rooms alongside extensive gardens. The property's location, tucked into a peaceful valley, provides perfect base exploring nearby Loire River activities.

Rooms feature period furnishings collected by three generations of the current family. Breakfasts served in the formal dining room or garden terrace introduce regional specialties while facilitating conversation with fellow guests. The hosts excel at arranging authentic experiences: truffle hunting in winter, garden workshops in spring, grape harvesting in autumn.

Le Petit Moulin (78 Rue du Moulin, Chaumont-sur-Loire; +33 2 54 20 98 98; gîte from €720 weekly) transforms a miller's house into cozy accommodation. Situated beside a restored water wheel and requiring vehicle access from Blois (15 kilometers), this charming property sleeps six through three bedrooms. The location, walking distance from Chaumont's famous château and garden festival, combines rural tranquility with cultural access.

The renovation preserves industrial heritage elements while ensuring modern comfort. The original mill mechanism remains visible through glass floor sections, while the wheel still turns during high water periods. The fully-equipped kitchen encourages local market shopping, though excellent restaurants lie within walking distance.

Practical considerations shape rural stays. Personal transportation proves essential reaching properties and exploring surroundings. Shopping requires planning around village store hours and market days. Language barriers might arise in rural settings, though most hosts manage basic English communication.

Seasonal activities enhance countryside experiences. Spring brings lambing season and garden planting. Summer enables outdoor dining and swimming. Autumn features grape and mushroom harvesting. Winter offers truffle hunting and traditional preserving activities. Many properties maintain detailed activity calendars helping guests plan participation.

Cultural understanding enriches rural stays. Traditional greeting customs remain important in countryside settings. Meal times typically follow French patterns: late lunches, evening dining after 7:30. Many properties host occasional communal meals allowing natural interaction between guests and locals.

These remarkable properties preserve Loire Valley rural heritage while creating thoroughly modern holiday experiences. Whether gathering eggs from property chickens, learning traditional recipes from host families, or discovering local wine-making traditions, rural stays offer authentic connections with French country life.

The experience transcends typical vacation rentals through deep immersion in local culture and traditions. Each property maintains unique character through careful preservation choices and thoughtful hosting, creating perfect bases exploring Loire Valley's rural heart.

Camping and Glamping Options

The Loire Valley's natural beauty beckons outdoor enthusiasts through remarkable camping and glamping experiences. These accommodations range from traditional riverside tent pitches through luxury safari-style lodges, each offering unique perspectives on France's garden.

Camping de l'Île d'Or (45 Rue de la Plage, Amboise; +33 2 47 57 09 39; tent pitches from €18, glamping pods from €85) claims prime position on Amboise's river island. Accessible via pedestrian bridge from Amboise station (10-minute walk), this municipal site combines natural beauty with urban convenience. The campground maintains 100 grass pitches beneath mature plane trees, while eight contemporary glamping pods offer elevated comfort.

Facilities reflect French camping excellence: immaculate shower blocks feature individual cubicles with reliable hot water, while the communal kitchen provides cooking stations with refrigeration. The site's riverside beach creates perfect swimming and sunbathing spots, while direct château views enhance evening relaxation. Reception staff arrange bicycle rentals and canoe excursions, simplifying Loire Valley exploration.

Loire Valley Luxury Camping (225 Route des Vignes, Chaumont-sur-Loire; +33 2 54 20 98 98; safari tents from €125, tree houses from €165) elevates outdoor living through sophisticated design. Located within walking distance of Chaumont's famous gardens and requiring car access from Blois, this boutique site limits accommodation to 15 upscale units ensuring peaceful atmosphere.

Safari-style tents feature proper beds with quality linens, en-suite bathrooms, and private decks perfect stargazing. Tree houses perched 6-8 meters high provide magical château views while maintaining full comfort through clever design. The site's restaurant serves excellent regional cuisine using local ingredients, while the heated pool offers welcome relaxation between château visits.

Camping du Val de Loire (78 Route de Tours, Langeais; +33 2 47 96 43 43; tent pitches from €15, mobile homes from €65) exemplifies traditional family camping. Situated beside Langeais forest and reached via combination of train to Langeais plus short taxi ride, this expansive site offers varied accommodation options across 150 pitches.

Excellent facilities include modern sanitary blocks, laundry stations, and well-equipped camp kitchen. The site shop stocks camping essentials alongside local products, while the snack bar serves simple meals during peak season. Children particularly enjoy the swimming pool complex and adventure playground, while parents appreciate direct access to forest walking trails.

Les Cabanes de Loire (156 Chemin des Mariniers, Saint-Dyé-sur-Loire; +33 2 54 81 60 60; riverside cabins from €145) specializes in waterfront glamping. Requiring personal transport from Blois, this intimate site features 12 architect-designed cabins positioned along a peaceful Loire tributary. Each unit combines rustic charm with modern comfort through careful design and premium materials.

The cabins incorporate extensive glazing maximizing river views while maintaining privacy through clever positioning. Full bathrooms and kitchenettes enable independent living, though the excellent site restaurant tempts many guests. The property's private river beach provides perfect launching kayak adventures, while partnerships with local wine makers create memorable tasting experiences.

Practical considerations shape outdoor stays. Advance booking proves essential during peak season (June-September), particularly regarding glamping options. Many sites close between November-March, though some maintain year-round glamping units. Personal transportation enhances exploration possibilities, though several sites offer good public transport connections.

French camping regulations ensure high standards through strict facility requirements. All sites maintain clearly marked emergency procedures and provide staff contact numbers. Environmental consciousness remains paramount - guests must respect quiet hours (typically 22:30-07:00) and follow waste sorting guidelines.

Weather significantly influences camping experiences. Spring brings mild temperatures perfect tent camping alongside spectacular wildflower displays. Summer enables full facility enjoyment though advance booking becomes crucial. Autumn offers peaceful atmosphere and beautiful colors while winter glamping provides unique perspective on Loire Valley life.

These diverse properties create perfect bases exploring regional attractions. Whether waking to château views from comfortable safari tents, discovering riverside wildlife from traditional pitches, or stargazing from architect-designed cabins, outdoor accommodation offers unique Loire Valley perspectives.

The experience transcends simple camping through thoughtful design and excellent facilities. Each site maintains distinct character while ensuring guest comfort, preservation of natural environments, and authentic connections with Loire Valley heritage.

Sustainable Stays

The Loire Valley's commitment to environmental stewardship shines through remarkable accommodations where sustainability meets luxury. These pioneering properties demonstrate how thoughtful design and careful operations preserve natural resources while creating extraordinary guest experiences.

L'Éco-Domaine des Roses (156 Route de la Loire, Montlouis-sur-Loire; +33 2 47 50 77 77; rooms from €165) stands proudly certified by Europe's rigorous EU Ecolabel program. Located amid organic vineyards and reached via combination of train to Montlouis station plus hotel's electric shuttle, this renovated wine estate demonstrates comprehensive sustainability through innovative systems.

Solar panels and geothermal heating meet energy needs while rainwater harvesting supplies garden irrigation. The property's 20 rooms incorporate locally-sourced materials: limestone walls from regional quarries, oak furniture crafted by Loire Valley artisans, and organic linens woven in Tours. The restaurant maintains zero-kilometer philosophy through estate-grown produce and partnerships with neighboring organic farms.

La Maison Passive (78 Rue des Vignerons, Vouvray; +33 2 47 52 88 88; rooms from €145) achieves remarkable energy efficiency through passive house design principles. This modern property, requiring car access from Tours, demonstrates how contemporary architecture can minimize environmental impact while maximizing comfort. Eight rooms utilize natural heating and cooling through strategic window placement and superior insulation.

The building's innovative design maintains comfortable temperatures year-round with minimal energy input. Living walls purify indoor air while providing fresh herbs kitchen use. The breakfast room features educational displays explaining passive house principles, inspiring guests consider sustainable building practices.

Château Vert (225 Chemin des Sources, Azay-le-Rideau; +33 2 47 45 99 99; rooms from €195) proves historic properties can achieve modern sustainability standards. This 18th-century château, accessible via Azay-le-Rideau station plus hotel's biodiesel shuttle, combines careful preservation with environmental innovation. Twelve rooms balance period authenticity with ecological responsibility through thoughtful renovation.

The property maintains extensive organic gardens supplying 80% restaurant ingredients while composting all organic waste. A sophisticated water management system combines historic rain cisterns with modern filtration technology. The château's thermal mass naturally regulates temperature, supplemented by renewable energy systems hidden within preserved architecture.

L'Auberge Écologique (45 Route des Bois, Chambord; +33 2 54 20 66 66; rooms from €155) creates sustainable luxury through small-scale operations. Requiring personal transport from Blois, this intimate property demonstrates how limited size enables maximum environmental consciousness. Six rooms occupy a restored forester's lodge surrounded by protected woodland.

Every aspect emphasizes sustainability: furniture pieces tell stories of reclaimed materials, while bathroom amenities come from local organic producers. The property's electric bicycle fleet encourages low-impact exploration, while partnerships with regional nature guides create memorable eco-tourism experiences.

Practical considerations enhance sustainable stays. Properties typically provide detailed guidance helping guests minimize environmental impact through water conservation, proper waste sorting, and energy-conscious behaviors. Many offer incentives encouraging sustainable choices: discounts refusing daily room cleaning, rewards using public transport or bicycles.

Environmental certifications indicate commitment levels. EU Ecolabel certification requires meeting strict criteria across operations. La Clef Verte (Green Key) focuses specifically on tourism sustainability. Numerous properties maintain additional organic and fair-trade certifications regarding food service.

Seasonal programming enhances environmental awareness. Spring brings guided walks identifying edible plants and traditional medicinal herbs. Summer enables full enjoyment sustainable outdoor activities including solar-powered boat tours. Autumn features harvest participation opportunities while winter highlights renewable energy systems' effectiveness.

These remarkable properties demonstrate sustainable tourism's vital role preserving Loire Valley heritage. Whether experiencing passive solar design, discovering organic farming practices, or exploring protected environments, guests contribute directly toward regional conservation efforts.

The sustainable experience transcends simple environmental consciousness through deep connection with Loire Valley ecosystems. Each property maintains unique approach toward sustainability while ensuring guest comfort and authentic cultural experiences, creating perfect balance between preservation and hospitality.

Chapter 8: Practical Information

Transportation Network

The gentle morning mist rises over the Loire River as travelers emerge from Paris Montparnasse station, stepping onto French soil that has witnessed centuries of royal passages. The modern TGV network transforms this historical journey into a swift 1-hour sprint from Paris, reaching speeds of 320 kilometers per hour across France's heartland. Regional express trains branch outward like medieval trade routes, connecting châteaux towns through a sophisticated rail system that would have amazed the Loire Valley's ancient inhabitants.

Standing at Tours Central Station, medieval architecture blends seamlessly with contemporary digital displays. Here, the SNCF's regional services weave together smaller communes - Amboise, Blois, and Chambord - in a ballet of punctual departures and arrivals. Each station tells its own story; Blois-Chambord station whispers tales of royal hunting parties while serving modern travelers with automated ticket machines and real-time journey planners.

The region's bus network complements rail services with remarkable precision. Rémi buses traverse routes both popular and hidden, reaching remote vineyards and lesser-known châteaux. These services peak during summer months when lavender fields bloom and tourists flock to famous castles. Winter brings a quieter rhythm, though services maintain their reliability, adapting schedules to local needs rather than tourist demands.

Imagine cycling along the Loire à Vélo route, part of an extensive bike-sharing network that spans 900 kilometers through the valley. Local authorities have integrated these systems with train services, allowing cyclists to combine modes of transport effortlessly. Bike stations dot city centers and tourist hotspots, their solar-powered terminals offering quick rentals through smartphone apps.

River transport adds another layer to this intricate network. Modern river cruises echo centuries-old trade vessels, offering both practical transport between riverside châteaux and romantic sunset journeys. These services operate from April through October, providing unique perspectives of riverside castles and villages that road travelers might miss.

Renting a car unveils different dimensions of the Loire Valley. Electric charging stations have proliferated across the region, while historic town centers increasingly restrict vehicle access to preserve their medieval character. Parking facilities near major châteaux have evolved, with intelligent systems guiding visitors to available spaces during peak seasons. However, summer months demand early arrival at popular sites like Chambord and Chenonceau.

The digital revolution has transformed ticket purchasing. The SNCF Connect app serves as a comprehensive travel companion, offering real-time updates and multi-modal journey planning. Regional transport cards like LibertéPlus provide significant savings for frequent travelers, while tourist passes combine transport with château entry tickets, reflecting the region's commitment to integrated tourism.

Accessibility has received considerable attention. Major stations feature elevator access and dedicated assistance services, though smaller stations might require advance arrangement. Many buses now kneel to curb level, while some châteaux operate specialized transport services for visitors with mobility challenges.

Transportation hubs have evolved into more than mere transit points. Tours station's renovation embraces both functionality and aesthetics, hosting local produce markets and cultural exhibitions. Information centers provide multilingual assistance, while digital displays track departures in real-time, creating stress-free travel environments.

Summer brings special shuttle services connecting major hotels with popular châteaux, operating on timetables aligned with château opening hours. These services reduce parking pressure at popular sites while offering guided commentary about passing landscapes and historical sites.

The Loire Valley's transportation network reflects both preservation and progress. While maintaining connections with its historical roots, the system embraces technological advances and environmental consciousness. From high-speed rail to electric bikes, from river cruises to accessible buses, the network serves diverse needs while respecting the valley's cultural heritage.

Success lies in understanding this transportation tapestry. Planning ahead, especially during peak seasons, ensures smooth journeys. Digital tools simplify navigation, while integrated tickets maximize value. Most importantly, the network allows travelers to experience the Loire Valley's magnificence at their own pace, creating personal journeys through this UNESCO World Heritage landscape.

The future promises further evolution - increased electric mobility, enhanced digital integration, and continued emphasis on sustainable transport. Yet the essence remains unchanged: providing access to centuries of history while preserving the valley's timeless charm for future generations.

Language Tips

Between cobblestone streets and ancient château walls, French words dance like autumn leaves in the Loire Valley's gentle breeze. Learning these linguistic steps transforms mere tourism into genuine cultural immersion. Picture yourself beneath Chambord's imposing spires, where every "Bonjour" opens doors to authentic connections, and each "Merci" weaves threads of local appreciation.

Morning markets buzz with essential French phrases. "C'est combien?" (How much?) floats between stalls of fresh produce, while "Je voudrais..." (I would like...) helps secure perfectly ripened cheese. Regional accents add distinctive flavors - Loire Valley French carries subtle differences from Parisian pronunciation, particularly in words describing wine and castle architecture.

Wine tasting rooms demand their own vocabulary ballet. "Dégustation" (tasting) begins conversations, while descriptive terms paint sensory pictures: "charpenté" (full-bodied), "léger" (light), "fruité" (fruity). Local vignerons appreciate visitors who embrace these terms, often responding with warmer, more detailed explanations of their craft. The phrase "Quelle est votre spécialité?" (What's your specialty?) typically unlocks passionate discussions about terroir and tradition.

Restaurant interactions require careful attention to cultural nuance. Always begin with "Bonjour Madame/Monsieur" - skipping this greeting marks visitors immediately. "Je n'ai pas réservé" (I don't have a reservation) might save embarrassment during busy seasons. Regional specialties deserve special linguistic care: "rillettes" (meat spread) and "fouace" (local bread) challenge English-speaking tongues but reward proper pronunciation with server appreciation.

Château tours reveal another language layer. "Visite guidée" (guided tour) and "audioguide" become essential tools. Understanding basic architectural terms enriches experiences: "escalier" (staircase), "donjon" (keep), and "chapelle" (chapel). Mobile apps like France Heritage enhance vocabulary through interactive château descriptions, while Forvo provides native pronunciation examples.

Cultural formality levels shape social interactions. "Vous" (formal you) shows respect when addressing older residents or service professionals. "Tu" (informal you) risks offense unless explicitly invited. "Excusez-moi" (excuse me) opens conversations politely, while "S'il vous plaît" and "Merci beaucoup" demonstrate courtesy that Loire Valley residents deeply value.

Emergency situations require clear communication. Memorize "J'ai besoin d'un médecin" (I need a doctor) and "Appelez les pompiers" (Call the fire department). Local pharmacies understand "J'ai mal à..." (I have pain in...), followed by pointing. Police stations recognize "J'ai perdu..." (I've lost...) or "On m'a volé..." (I've been robbed...).

Transportation vocabulary smooths daily movement. "Aller-retour" (round trip) and "correspondance" (connection) prove vital at train stations. Bus stops require understanding "prochain arrêt" (next stop) and "terminus" (final destination). Taxi conversations flow better with "Pourriez-vous m'emmener à..." (Could you take me to...).

Mobile technology bridges remaining gaps. Google Translate's camera function deciphers menus and signs instantly. DeepL provides more nuanced translations, particularly helpful when reading historical plaques or museum descriptions. Language exchange apps connect travelers with local speakers, creating opportunities to practice before arrival.

Regional expressions color conversations distinctly. "Ça caille!" (It's freezing!) reflects Loire Valley winters, while "Être en goguette" describes festive moments. These phrases, when appropriately used, spark genuine smiles from locals who appreciate efforts to embrace regional character.

Accommodation interactions benefit from specific phrases. "La climatisation ne marche pas" (The air conditioning isn't working) and "La chambre est bruyante" (The room is noisy) address common issues clearly. "Pouvez-vous recommander...?" (Can you recommend...?) often leads to valuable local insights from hotel staff.

Success in Loire Valley communication stems from combining basic French skills with cultural awareness and digital tools. Preparation matters - downloading offline translation apps and practicing key phrases before arrival creates confidence. Yet most importantly, maintaining a humble, appreciative approach toward language learning transforms potential barriers into bridges of cultural understanding.

Money Matters

Beneath the Loire Valley's regal façades lies a practical world of modern financial considerations. Picture standing before an ornate château ticket counter, sunlight streaming through medieval windows, while contemplating the seamless blend of historical grandeur and contemporary payment systems. This financial landscape shapes every traveler's experience, from morning croissants to evening wine tastings.

Digital payments dominate urban areas and major attractions. Contactless cards spark to life at château entrances, while Apple Pay and Google Wallet simplify transactions in Tours' bustling markets. Yet rural charm brings practical considerations - small village boulangeries and local vignerons might warmly request cash payments, their traditions extending beyond mere commerce to preserve personal connections with customers.

Banking services cluster around transportation hubs and historic centers. Major French banks - Crédit Agricole, BNP Paribas, Société Générale - maintain prominent presence in cities like Tours, Blois, and Orléans. International travelers find refuge in these financial oases, where multilingual ATMs dispense euros beneath centuries-old architecture. Smart travelers withdraw larger sums less frequently, minimizing international transaction fees while maintaining security through hotel safes.

Credit card acceptance varies meaningfully across establishments. High-end restaurants and luxury hotels embrace international cards, though American Express sees limited acceptance compared to Visa and Mastercard. Smaller establishments, particularly in remote villages, prefer cash or local bank cards. Wise travelers carry both payment forms, understanding that each transaction method opens different doors to authentic experiences.

Tipping customs reflect French cultural nuances. Restaurant service charges (15%) appear automatically on bills, marked as "service compris." Additional gratuities remain optional but appreciated - leaving coins or rounding up bills demonstrates appreciation without obligation. Tour guides, particularly at private châteaux, welcome tips of €10-20 per group, while hotel porters expect €1-2 per bag. These gestures build bridges between cultures while respecting local customs.

Tax refund procedures reward strategic shopping. Purchases exceeding €100 in qualified stores qualify for VAT refunds, transforming Loire Valley wine collections and artisanal souvenirs into savvy investments. Experienced travelers collect necessary documentation during purchases, then process refunds at major train stations or airports before departure, avoiding last-minute complications.

Budgeting strategies span diverse travel styles. Luxury seekers might allocate €300-400 daily for château-hotel accommodations and Michelin-starred dining experiences. Mid-range travelers find comfort at €150-200 daily, balancing charming bed-and-breakfasts with local restaurants. Budget-conscious explorers thrive on €80-100 daily through hostel stays and market-sourced picnics beneath château spires.

Daily expense management requires thoughtful planning. Morning markets offer fresh provisions at local prices, while tourist-area restaurants command premium rates. Transportation costs vary - regional trains between châteaux prove more economical than private tours, though guided experiences often justify their expense through deeper historical insights and exclusive access.

Financial security demands attention amid historic distractions. Pickpockets occasionally target crowded tourist sites, particularly during peak season. Prudent travelers separate funds between secure hotel safes and daily carrying amounts, while maintaining digital copies of important documents. Emergency contact numbers for major banks remain readily accessible, though rarely needed in this generally secure region.

Modern financial technology simplifies travel logistics. Mobile banking apps provide instant transaction notifications and currency conversion, while services like Wise offer competitive exchange rates through multi-currency accounts. These digital tools free travelers to focus on experiences rather than calculations.

Seasonal considerations influence costs significantly. Peak summer months command premium prices for accommodations and experiences, while shoulder seasons (April-May, September-October) offer similar charm at reduced rates. Winter travelers discover exceptional value, though some attractions operate limited hours.

Financial emergencies find resolution through established channels. Major banks maintain English-speaking emergency services, while tourist police stations handle financial crime reports efficiently. Travel insurance provides additional peace of mind, particularly when covering expensive château hotel reservations or premium wine purchases.

Success in Loire Valley financial management combines preparation with flexibility. Understanding payment preferences, respecting tipping customs, and maintaining security awareness creates space for spontaneous moments. Most importantly, thoughtful financial planning allows travelers to embrace the region's magic without constant monetary concerns, transforming practical considerations into stepping stones toward unforgettable experiences.

Shopping Guide

Dawn mists swirl around medieval market squares where centuries of commerce echo through cobblestone streets. Shopping in Loire Valley transcends mere transactions - each purchase weaves stories of artisanal heritage and regional pride into travelers' memories. Morning light reveals local markets springing to life, their wooden stalls groaning under fresh produce, artisanal cheeses, and handcrafted delicacies.

Markets paint vibrant portraits of regional life. Tours' central market radiates authenticity, its halls filled with passionate vendors showcasing generations-old recipes and techniques. Bargaining remains subtle here - building rapport through appreciation and curiosity often yields better prices than aggressive negotiation. Market timing proves crucial: early mornings bring the freshest selections, while late afternoons might reveal discounted treasures.

Wine purchasing demands thoughtful consideration. Beyond famous châteaux cellars, independent vignerons welcome visitors to intimate tasting rooms where passion flows freely alongside premier vintages. Shipping logistics shape buying decisions - specialized wine-shipping services ensure bottles reach home safely, handling customs documentation and temperature-controlled transport. Smart collectors maintain detailed purchase records, facilitating smooth customs declarations while documenting their Loire Valley wine journey.

Artisanal crafts tell stories through skilled hands. Traditional workshops scattered throughout the valley preserve centuries-old techniques in pottery, glasswork, and textile production. Authentication certificates accompany genuine pieces, while apprenticeship lineages trace artistic heritage. Shipping fragile items requires specialized services - experienced artisans partner with trusted shippers, ensuring cherished purchases survive their journeys home.

Shopping hours reflect French cultural rhythms. Most shops welcome customers Tuesday through Saturday, 9:30-19:00, though lunch breaks (12:30-14:30) remain sacred in smaller towns. Sunday trading flourishes in designated tourist zones near major châteaux, while other areas observe traditional closing. National holidays bring complete closures, though tourist-focused shops might maintain limited hours.

Seasonal sales periods transform shopping landscapes. Winter sales (early January) and summer sales (late June) slash prices dramatically, particularly on fashion and home goods. Strategic shoppers arrive early, understanding premium items disappear quickly. Between official sales periods, independent shops might offer discrete discounts, especially during shoulder seasons.

Luxury retail clusters around historic centers. International brands claim restored medieval buildings, their modern displays contrasting beautifully with ancient stonework. Local boutiques showcase regional designers, their unique interpretations of Loire Valley elegance commanding premium prices justified by exceptional craftsmanship.

Tax refund procedures reward strategic shopping. Purchases exceeding €100 qualify when made in participating stores, identifiable by "Tax Free Shopping" signage. Savvy travelers collect refund documentation throughout their journey, processing claims at departure points. Digital refund systems streamline processes, though paper forms remain common in smaller establishments.

Themed shopping routes reveal local character. Tours' Old Town pairs antique hunting with gastronomic discoveries, while Blois emphasizes artisanal crafts. Amboise excels in wine-related souvenirs, its shops offering everything from professional tasting equipment to decorative cork art. These routes provide structure while leaving room spontaneous discoveries.

Export considerations shape purchasing decisions. Wine shipments require detailed documentation, including proof purchase and origin certificates. Fragile items need specialized packing services, available through dedicated shipping stores in major towns. Smart travelers research import restrictions before committing to significant purchases.

Shopping authenticity requires educated eyes. Genuine regional products carry protected designation labels - AOC/AOP certifications guarantee wine origins, while artisanal crafts display maker's marks and authentication certificates. Price variations between similar items often reflect these quality guarantees.

Success in Loire Valley shopping combines preparation with spontaneity. Understanding trading hours, sale periods, and export requirements creates space authentic discoveries. Digital payment readiness pairs with cash availability, ensuring no opportunity slips away. Most importantly, approaching each purchase with curiosity and respect transforms shopping into cultural exploration, creating memories that enrich long after returning home.

The valley's commercial spirit lives through its modern merchants, each transaction adding new chapters to millennia of trading history. Between grand château boutiques and humble market stalls lies the heart of Loire Valley commerce - a blend of tradition and innovation, quality and authenticity, where every purchase tells a story worth bringing home.

Health and Safety

Morning sunlight streams through château windows, illuminating centuries of architectural splendor - yet behind this romantic façade lies a modern healthcare system ready to support travelers through any challenge. The French medical network extends its excellence throughout the Loire Valley, where historic towns house state-of-the-art clinics and centuries-old pharmacies dispense contemporary care.

Healthcare access begins with understanding emergency numbers: 15 reaches medical services (SAMU), 17 connects to police, while 18 summons firefighters. The European-wide 112 brings multi-lingual emergency response. These numbers function without cellular service or SIM cards, providing constant safety connections. Local pharmacies, marked by green crosses, serve minor health needs and offer multilingual staff trained to bridge cultural gaps.

Hospitals in major towns - Tours, Orléans, Blois - maintain international patient services, accepting European Health Insurance Cards and major international insurance plans. Private clinics provide faster access, though public hospitals deliver equivalent care quality. Emergency rooms (urgences) never refuse treatment, regardless of insurance status, though having coverage prevents financial stress during medical events.

Travel insurance considerations stretch beyond basic medical coverage. Comprehensive plans should include emergency evacuation, particularly valuable when exploring remote vineyards or cycling distant château routes. Coverage verification before departure ensures policy validity in France, while understanding claim procedures prevents administrative headaches during emergencies.

Activity-specific safety demands attention. Loire à Vélo cyclists encounter varied terrain - securing proper equipment from certified rental shops while maintaining hydration prevents common injuries. Water activities along the Loire River require respecting posted warnings and seasonal conditions. Château visits, though generally safe, benefit from comfortable footwear and attention to historic staircases.

Weather preparedness shapes daily planning. Summer heat necessitates regular hydration and sun protection, particularly during château garden tours or market visits. Spring and autumn rains transform cobblestone streets into slippery surfaces, demanding careful navigation. Winter brings occasional ice, though main thoroughfares receive prompt treatment.

Food safety reflects French cultural pride. Market vendors maintain strict hygiene standards, though perishable purchases require proper storage. Regional specialties - raw milk cheeses, charcuterie - come from regulated producers, balancing tradition with food safety. Restaurant hygiene standards rank among Europe's highest, while street food vendors display required certifications.

Medical condition management requires advance planning. Prescription medications should travel in original containers with copies of prescriptions using international nomenclature. Local pharmacies can usually match medications, though certain prescriptions might require physician consultation. Mobility challenges find increasing accommodation at major sites, though advance contact ensures appropriate arrangements.

Seasonal health considerations influence travel experiences. Spring allergies might affect château garden visits, while summer heat impacts cycling endurance. Medical facilities anticipate these seasonal patterns, adjusting services accordingly. Understanding personal health patterns helps match activities to individual capabilities.

Crime prevention relies mostly on common sense. Tourist areas maintain visible security, though standard precautions - securing valuables, maintaining awareness in crowds - enhance peace of mind. Evening safety benefits from well-lit main streets and reliable taxi services, while smaller towns provide naturally secure environments through community presence.

Physical preparation matches planned activities. Château tours involve numerous stairs, while cycling routes cover varied terrains. Realistic activity planning prevents overexertion, allowing enjoyment without exhaustion. Regular rest periods, particularly during summer heat, maintain energy levels while enriching experiences through relaxed observation.

Success in Loire Valley health management combines preparation with flexibility. Understanding emergency procedures while maintaining appropriate insurance creates confidence to explore freely. Local medical professionals pride themselves on maintaining their region's reputation through excellent care. Most importantly, balancing ambition with personal limits ensures memorable experiences unmarred by preventable health challenges.

The Loire Valley's charm lies partly in its ability to blend historical grandeur with modern safety infrastructure. Between ancient walls and contemporary clinics, travelers find security in knowing world-class care stands ready, allowing full immersion in the region's timeless appeal without compromising wellbeing.

Sustainable Tourism Practices

Dawn breaks over misty vineyards where centuries of agricultural wisdom meet modern environmental consciousness. The Loire Valley stands at a pivotal moment - balancing its timeless appeal with pressing sustainability needs. Through mindful choices, travelers become stewards of this UNESCO World Heritage landscape, protecting its magic while deepening their connection to its living heritage.

Environmental consciousness begins with transportation decisions. Electric trains glide between major destinations, producing minimal carbon emissions while offering panoramic valley views. Regional electric bus networks complement rail services, while bicycle routes trace ancient paths between châteaux. These eco-friendly options reveal hidden perspectives - morning mists rising over vineyards, locals tending heritage gardens, wildlife stirring in protected habitats.

Château visits embrace sustainability through thoughtful timing. Early morning arrivals avoid peak crowds, reducing strain on historic structures while creating intimate experiences with these architectural treasures. Many châteaux now implement timed entry systems, protecting delicate ecosystems within their gardens while ensuring each visitor experiences their majesty fully. Supporting these preservation efforts through authorized guided tours channels tourism revenue directly into conservation.

Local economies thrive through intentional spending patterns. Small-scale vignerons practicing sustainable viticulture welcome visitors to intimate tasting sessions, sharing generations of expertise while protecting traditional methods. Family-run restaurants source ingredients from nearby farms, maintaining agricultural diversity while offering authentic flavors. Artisanal craftspeople preserve heritage skills, transforming local materials into lasting treasures through sustainable practices.

Accommodation choices shape environmental impact significantly. Historic buildings renovated into eco-conscious hotels blend modern efficiency with traditional charm. Rural gîtes operated by local families offer immersive experiences while supporting community economies. Many establishments now highlight their sustainability initiatives - solar power, water conservation, waste reduction - allowing travelers to align lodging choices with environmental values.

Photography practices require cultural sensitivity. While châteaux exteriors welcome photography, interior restrictions protect delicate artifacts from harmful flash exposure. Responsible social media sharing raises awareness about preservation needs while respecting local privacy preferences.

Many sites now designate specific photo points, balancing visitor desires with conservation requirements.

Cultural preservation extends beyond physical structures. Local festivals celebrating regional traditions deserve respectful participation rather than mere observation. Learning basic French phrases demonstrates cultural appreciation, while patient interaction with local residents builds meaningful connections. These efforts maintain the valley's living heritage, ensuring traditions pass to future generations.

Water conservation takes particular importance in this riverine landscape. Hotels increasingly offer incentives reducing towel changes, while restaurants proudly serve tap water, highlighting the region's excellent water quality. River tours emphasize ecosystem protection, teaching visitors about the Loire's crucial role in regional biodiversity.

Waste reduction shapes daily choices. Reusable water bottles filled from public fountains eliminate plastic waste while connecting travelers to historic water sources. Market shopping with cloth bags supports local producers while reducing packaging waste. Many restaurants now serve regional specialties in portions preventing food waste, encouraging mindful consumption of local delicacies.

Seasonal awareness enhances sustainability efforts. Visiting during shoulder seasons reduces environmental pressure while revealing different aspects of valley life. Spring and autumn trips catch comfortable temperatures ideal cycling weather, while winter visits showcase architectural details usually hidden by summer foliage.

Success in sustainable Loire Valley tourism requires balancing preservation with experience. Understanding how individual choices impact local communities creates opportunities meaningful contribution. Supporting businesses committed environmental stewardship ensures their continued operation, while spreading awareness encourages broader adoption of sustainable practices.

Between ancient stones and modern environmental challenges lies opportunity for transformative travel. Through conscious choices, visitors become participants in preserving this remarkable landscape, ensuring future generations will find same magic that draws travelers today. The Loire Valley's future depends on this delicate balance - protecting its heritage while sharing its treasures with mindful visitors.

Digital Resources and Apps

Ancient meets algorithm in the Loire Valley, where medieval spires rise alongside digital innovations. Smart devices transform into personal guides, translators, and cultural interpreters, bridging centuries through technology while preserving the region's timeless magic. The digital landscape enriches exploration, creating seamless experiences across historical domains.

Essential mobile applications shape modern Loire Valley experiences. The official Val de Loire app serves as digital compass, combining real-time château waiting times with augmented reality features revealing historical perspectives. Pointing devices at castle façades unveils architectural evolution, while garden walks trigger location-based stories about royal inhabitants and historical events.

Translation technology breaks language barriers effectively. DeepL captures cultural nuances better than traditional translation apps, particularly valuable when deciphering historical plaques or engaging local vignerons. Camera-based translation instantly decodes menus and signage, though learning basic French phrases still enriches human connections.

Château-specific applications enhance visitor engagement significantly. Chambord's dedicated app reveals hidden architectural details through 3D modeling, while Chenonceau's digital guide adapts content depth based on visitor interests. These platforms combine historical accuracy with multimedia storytelling, creating personalized exploration paths through vast historical complexes.

Mobile connectivity remains robust throughout populated areas. Major carriers - Orange, SFR, Bouygues - provide reliable 5G coverage across tourist regions. Local SIM cards offer competitive data rates, while international plans increasingly include French coverage. Public WiFi networks blanket city centers and major attractions, though rural areas might require offline preparation.

Digital booking platforms streamline travel logistics remarkably. SNCF Connect handles train reservations while integrating local transport options. Château Pass digital tickets eliminate physical queuing, storing entry rights securely within mobile wallets. Restaurant booking platforms like TheFork (LaFourchette) unlock tables at sought-after establishments, often securing exclusive dining discounts.

Social media engagement reveals real-time regional insights. Local tourism offices maintain active presence across platforms, sharing event updates and crowd conditions. Instagram location tags help discover photography opportunities and hidden viewpoints, while Facebook groups connect travelers with resident experts. These digital communities often share practical tips beyond traditional guidebook scope.

Weather applications merit special attention. Météo-France provides hyperlocal forecasts crucial cycling plans or garden visits. Agricultural weather services offer detailed precipitation predictions valuable wine tours or outdoor activities. Understanding these tools helps maximize favorable conditions while avoiding weather-related disappointments.

Digital documentation strategies preserve travel memories effectively. Google Photos automatically backs up images while creating location-based albums. Day Live compiles daily movements into shareable travel logs, while journal apps like Day encrypt personal reflections. These tools create lasting records without diminishing present-moment experiences.

Cybersecurity demands consistent attention during travels. VPN services protect sensitive data when using public WiFi networks. Password managers secure digital credentials, while two-factor authentication adds protection digital financial transactions. Regular backup routines safeguard travel documentation against device loss emergencies.

Mobile payment systems simplify financial transactions considerably. Digital wallets - Apple Pay, Google Pay - gain widespread acceptance, reducing cash carrying needs. Banking apps provide real-time currency conversion, while specialized platforms like Wise optimize international transactions. These tools streamline purchases while maintaining transaction records.

Success in digital Loire Valley exploration balances technology with tradition. Understanding available tools while maintaining human connections creates rich travel experiences. Offline preparation ensures technology enhances rather than dominates exploration. Most importantly, digital resources serve as bridges to deeper cultural understanding, not barriers between travelers and authentic experiences.

Between medieval stones and modern screens lies opportunity for enhanced discovery. Through thoughtful application of digital tools, travelers unlock deeper understanding of Loire Valley's treasures while maintaining meaningful connections to its living heritage. This digital evolution ensures the region's stories reach future generations while preserving their timeless essence.

Conclusion: Embracing the Loire Valley Spirit

Sunset bathes ancient limestone walls in golden light while evening mists rise from the Loire River, nature's daily tribute to this remarkable valley. Through centuries of artistic achievement, architectural innovation, and vinicultural mastery, the Loire Valley has crafted an identity transcending mere geography. Here, between flowing waters and soaring spires, past and present dance eternally.

The valley reveals itself slowly, like a fine Vouvray wine opening in the glass. Each château tells multiple stories - through grand architectural statements, through intimate garden paths, through whispered legends of royal intrigue. Chambord's double-helix staircase spirals through time, while Chenonceau's gallery floating above the Cher River demonstrates human ambition harmonizing with natural beauty. These monuments stand not as museum pieces but living chapters in an ongoing cultural narrative.

Vineyards carpet hillsides where Roman legions once marched and medieval monks first cultivated noble grapes. Modern vignerons maintain ancient wisdom while embracing innovative techniques, producing wines that speak eloquently of specific soils, climates, and traditions. Each glass poured in a candlelit cave or sun-dappled tasting room connects drinkers to generations of agricultural expertise.

Medieval towns preserve their authenticity while embracing contemporary life. Markets still buzz with morning commerce, locals debating the ripeness of cherries or the perfect age of cheese. Narrow streets wind between half-timbered houses where artisans practice centuries-old crafts using traditional methods. Yet these same streets host modern art galleries, innovative restaurants, and cultural festivals bridging historical roots with creative futures.

Gardens demonstrate the valley's mastery of designed nature. Formal parterres at Villandry celebrate geometric precision, while wilder spaces at Chaumont's International Garden Festival push horticultural boundaries. These green spaces reflect changing relationships between humans and environment, from displays of Renaissance power to modern ecological awareness.

The Loire River itself remains central protagonist, shaping commerce, agriculture, and daily life since prehistoric times. Its waters mirror château facades while nurturing rich biodiversity. Modern kayakers follow ancient trade routes, while cycling paths along its banks connect communities just as river commerce once did. This mighty waterway continues inspiring artists, engineers, and dreamers.

Cultural preservation efforts ensure future generations will experience this heritage. Restoration projects employ traditional crafts alongside modern techniques, maintaining historical authenticity while strengthening structural integrity. Sustainable tourism initiatives balance access with protection, recognizing that experiencing beauty creates advocates its preservation.

Local communities maintain living traditions through seasonal celebrations, culinary arts, and cultural festivals. Weekly markets preserve social bonds while supporting regional producers. Wine festivals celebrate harvests while passing viticultural knowledge between generations. These traditions evolve naturally, remaining relevant while honoring their origins.

Experiencing Loire Valley transforms travelers subtly yet permanently. Knowledge of wine deepens beyond mere taste appreciation into understanding terroir's profound influence. Architectural awareness expands beyond style recognition into grasping how buildings shape human experience. Cultural perspectives broaden through direct engagement with living traditions.

The valley's future builds upon this rich foundation. Climate change adaptation efforts protect vulnerable ecosystems while sustainable tourism practices ensure monument preservation. Digital interpretation tools enhance understanding without diminishing direct experience. These initiatives demonstrate how thoughtful development can strengthen rather than diminish heritage value.

Taking home Loire Valley spirit means carrying forward its lessons about harmony between human achievement and natural beauty. Understanding how past generations shaped their world inspires thoughtful consideration about shaping our own. Appreciating fine wine teaches patience and attention to subtle detail. Experiencing architectural masterpieces demonstrates how human creativity can elevate daily life.

The Loire Valley remains eternally relevant because it speaks to fundamental human desires - creating beauty, preserving heritage, celebrating life's pleasures. Between its châteaux and vineyards, markets and gardens, flows an eternal spirit of cultural achievement and joie de vivre. This spirit touches every thoughtful visitor, ensuring the valley's magic lives on through transformed perspectives and enriched understanding.

Appendices

Annual Event Calendar

The Loire Valley pulses with cultural vitality throughout the year, each season bringing unique celebrations that transform this UNESCO landscape into a living theater of traditions. Between ancient château walls and rolling vineyards, festivals mark time's passage while connecting present celebrations to centuries of heritage.

January opens quietly, medieval towns glowing with lingering holiday illuminations. Tours' Circus Festival (January 15-28) brings contemporary performances to historic venues, while smaller communities celebrate Three Kings Day through traditional galette des rois sharing ceremonies. Early booking secures prime circus show seats, while local bakeries require advance galette orders.

February warms spirits through cultural celebrations. Chinon's Medieval Carnival (February 8-11) fills narrow streets with costumed revelers, while Amboise hosts its Truffle and Wine Festival (February 22-24). Carnival participation improves with period costume rental, available through local historical societies. Truffle hunting demonstrations require advance registration.

March heralds spring through garden celebrations. Chaumont-sur-Loire's International Garden Festival (March 15 - November 3) showcases innovative landscape design. Villandry's first garden tours resume, revealing early blooms against restored Renaissance patterns. Morning visits avoid crowds, while afternoon light creates superior photography conditions.

April bursts with Easter celebrations and flower festivals. Blois Castle's Easter Egg Hunt (April 7) transforms royal gardens into family adventure zones. Tours' Spring Wine Fair (April 19-21) presents new vintages from regional producers. Easter events sell out weeks ahead, while wine fair tickets include valuable tasting masterclasses.

May brings musical magic through château concerts. Chambord's Classical Music Festival (May 10-26) places world-class performances within architectural masterpieces. Amateur musicians gather harmonies through Regional Choir Festival (May 18-19). Concert packages including dinner reservations offer complete cultural evenings.

June celebrates river heritage through Loire Festival (June 14-16), recreating traditional boat launches while highlighting water conservation. Château gardens peak through Rose Festival celebrations, particularly magnificent at Chenonceau (June 21-23). River festival tickets include vintage boat rides, while rose events feature cultivation workshops.

July ignites summer entertainment. Tours' Summer in the Loire (July 1-31) brings street performances throughout historic districts. Bastille Day (July 14) celebrations illuminate château facades through spectacular fireworks. Street performance schedules appear weekly, while fireworks viewing requires strategic positioning knowledge.

August radiates harvest anticipation. Wine villages host street festivals, notably Saint-Aignan's Medieval Wine Festival (August 10-11). Chambord's Night Lights (August weekends) transform architecture through sound and light installations. Village festivals welcome spontaneous participation, while night shows demand advance booking.

September celebrates vintage through grape harvests and wine festivals. Vouvray's Grape Harvest Festival (September 7-8) invites public participation in traditional picking methods. Montlouis Wine Marathon (September 14) combines athletics with wine appreciation. Harvest participation requires early morning commitment, while marathon entries close months ahead.

October colors cultural landscapes through autumn festivals. Amboise's Historical Reenactment Weekend (October 5-6) brings Leonardo da Vinci's era alive. Regional mushroom festivals celebrate mycological treasures through guided forest walks. Historical costumes enhance reenactment experiences, while mushroom walks require expert guide booking.

November warms spirits through gastronomic celebrations. Tours' Gastronomic Festival (November 15-17) showcases regional culinary heritage. Thanksgiving markets in expatriate communities blend American traditions with Loire Valley products. Chef demonstrations require separate tickets, while market timing affects product selection.

December transforms medieval towns through Christmas markets and winter festivals. Blois Christmas Market (December 7-24) fills Place Louis XII with artisanal crafts. Château Christmas celebrations recreate historical winter traditions. Market visits improve through morning timing, while château events include special evening access.

These celebrations weave together into rich cultural fabric, each festival adding unique threads to Loire Valley's living heritage. Through thoughtful timing and advance planning, travelers participate fully in these timeless traditions while creating personal connections to this remarkable region's ongoing story.

Emergency Contacts and Healthcare Facilities

Between serene château gardens and bustling market squares lies a sophisticated healthcare network ready to support travelers through any emergency. Understanding these resources transforms potential crises into manageable situations, ensuring peace of mind while exploring this magnificent region.

Emergency numbers remain consistently accessible throughout France. The universal European emergency number 112 connects callers to multilingual operators capable of coordinating appropriate responses. Medical emergencies specifically require 15 (SAMU - Service d'Aide Médicale Urgente), while police assistance arrives through 17, and firefighters respond to 18. These numbers function without cellular service or SIM cards, providing constant safety connections.

Major hospitals anchor regional healthcare delivery. Tours University Hospital Center stands ready 24/7 with comprehensive emergency services and dedicated international patient liaison staff. Orléans Regional Hospital Complex provides similar coverage northward, while Blois Hospital Center serves central valley communities. These facilities maintain helicopter evacuation capabilities, crucial when emergencies occur near remote châteaux or vineyards.

English-speaking medical services cluster around tourist centers. Tours hosts numerous bilingual private clinics, their staff experienced with international insurance procedures. SOS Médecins provides 24/7 house calls throughout major towns, offering vital support when mobility becomes challenging. These services typically require credit card payment initially, with insurance reimbursement following standard procedures.

Pharmacies operate through coordinated networks ensuring 24-hour access. Green crosses indicate operating pharmacies, while electronic displays list current duty pharmacies handling after-hours needs. These professionals often provide first-line healthcare advice, helping distinguish between minor ailments requiring over-counter solutions and conditions demanding physician attention.

Medical communication benefits from prepared phrases. "J'ai besoin d'un médecin" (I need a doctor) opens conversations effectively, while "C'est urgent" (It's urgent) communicates immediacy. Pointing while saying "J'ai mal ici" (I have pain here) overcomes language barriers, though many medical professionals speak basic English.

Insurance procedures require understanding. European Health Insurance Cards facilitate public system access, while private international coverage typically needs upfront payment followed by reimbursement claims. Maintaining digital copies of insurance documentation streamlines admission procedures, while understanding policy coverage limits helps manage expectations.

Chronic condition management demands preparation. Carrying medication lists using international nomenclature helps local pharmacists identify equivalents when replacements become necessary. Letters from home physicians describing conditions in basic medical terminology facilitate communication with French healthcare providers. These documents prove invaluable during unexpected complications.

After-hours care follows structured protocols. Calling 15 connects patients with medical regulators who assess situations and direct appropriate responses. Night pharmacies maintain limited but essential inventories, while emergency dental services operate through regional scheduling systems. Understanding these protocols prevents unnecessary anxiety during nighttime health events.

Seasonal health considerations influence service availability. Summer heat waves activate special response protocols, while winter conditions might affect transportation to medical facilities. Tourist season brings increased English-speaking staff coverage, though core emergency services maintain year-round effectiveness.

Mental health support remains accessible through dedicated channels. SOS Help provides English-language crisis counseling by phone, while major hospitals maintain psychiatric emergency services. These resources prove particularly valuable when travel stress or isolation triggers emotional challenges.

Transportation options include dedicated medical services. Licensed medical transport companies provide non-emergency transfers, while ambulances respond through the 15 system. Many travel insurance policies cover medical transport costs, though verification before travel prevents surprise expenses.

Success in managing Loire Valley health situations stems from preparation and understanding. Knowing available resources while maintaining appropriate insurance creates confidence to explore freely. Local medical professionals take pride in preserving their region's reputation through excellent care. Most importantly, this healthcare network ensures travelers can embrace Loire Valley experiences fully, knowing support stands ready if needed.

Between ancient stones and modern medical facilities lies comprehensive health security. Through understanding these resources, travelers transform potential health challenges into manageable situations, ensuring their Loire Valley journey remains focused on cultural discovery rather than medical concerns.

Tourist Information Centers

Morning light streams through arched windows of Tours' central tourist office, where centuries of local expertise merge with modern digital services. These welcoming spaces transform from mere information points into gateways unlocking the Loire Valley's deepest treasures, staffed by passionate professionals eager to share their homeland's magic.

The Tours Tourist Information Center anchors regional tourism services from its prime location near the cathedral. Multilingual staff bring historical periods alive through carefully curated walking tours, while digital terminals provide instant access to accommodation bookings and transport schedules. Their specialized château desk crafts personalized itineraries matching individual interests with lesser-known architectural gems.

Amboise's tourist office occupies a restored medieval building, its stone walls housing cutting-edge visitor services. Leonardo da Vinci experts illuminate connections between the Renaissance genius and local landmarks, while wine tourism specialists arrange intimate tastings at family-owned vineyards. Their mobile app delivers real-time updates about château waiting times and special events.

Blois maintains multiple information points, strategically positioned near major attractions. The castle-adjacent office specializes in historical interpretation, offering period costume rentals and access to normally private château areas. Their river tourism desk coordinates kayak adventures and traditional boat excursions, while bicycle rental services facilitate Loire à Vélo route exploration.

Chambord's visitor center merges practical assistance with cultural education. Multimedia presentations reveal architectural secrets, while conservation experts share restoration insights during scheduled talks. Their events team handles exclusive evening access arrangements, transforming tourist inquiries into memorable experiences through insider knowledge.

Digital services extend information access beyond physical locations. Virtual concierge services provide pre-trip planning assistance through video calls, while mobile apps deliver real-time updates about local events and seasonal activities. These platforms connect travelers with local experts before arrival, enabling deeper destination understanding.

Seasonal programs reflect changing regional rhythms. Summer brings extended operating hours and additional walking tours, while winter services focus on indoor cultural experiences and festival planning. Spring and autumn programs highlight natural attractions, from garden tours to vineyard visits, adapting to weather conditions and cultural calendars.

Specialized desks cater to specific interests within larger offices. Gastronomic experts craft food-focused itineraries incorporating market visits and cooking classes, while outdoor adventure specialists map cycling routes through scenic landscapes. Photography desks identify prime shooting locations while sharing tips about optimal lighting conditions.

Booking services streamline travel logistics considerably. Staff leverage local connections securing tables at sought-after restaurants, while transportation coordinators arrange seamless transfers between attractions. Accommodation specialists match lodging options with specific needs, often accessing rooms unavailable through general booking platforms.

Language services break communication barriers effectively. Major offices maintain staff fluent in multiple languages, while smaller locations provide translation devices facilitating complex conversations. Cultural liaison officers help bridge understanding gaps, ensuring meaningful connections with local communities.

Emergency support remains constantly available through tourist office networks. After-hours hotlines connect travelers with assistance when physical locations close, while mobile response teams provide on-site support during major events. These services create security knowing help remains accessible throughout the region.

Success in utilizing tourist information resources stems from understanding their capabilities. Early contact enables thorough trip planning, while ongoing engagement reveals seasonal opportunities and special access possibilities. Most importantly, these centers transform from simple information sources into partners in discovery, their staff's passionate expertise illuminating paths toward authentic Loire Valley experiences.

Between historic walls and modern services lies accumulated wisdom ready to enhance every visit. Through thoughtful engagement with these resources, travelers unlock deeper understanding of Loire Valley treasures while creating connections that enrich their journey through this remarkable region.

Useful Phrases in French

Morning mist rises over château spires while the first "Bonjour" echoes through cobblestone streets, marking the beginning of linguistic adventures in Loire Valley. French phrases flow through daily experiences here, each interaction building bridges between cultures while deepening appreciation of regional heritage.

Essential greetings shape first impressions profoundly. "Bonjour" (good day) serves until sunset, when "Bonsoir" (good evening) takes over. Adding "Madame," "Monsieur," or "Mademoiselle" demonstrates respect, while "Au revoir" closes interactions gracefully. These courtesies, pronounced with genuine warmth, open doors throughout the region.

Château visits demand specific vocabulary mastery. "Billet d'entrée" (entrance ticket) starts exploration, while "visite guidée" (guided tour) enhances understanding. Historical terms enrich experiences: "escalier" (staircase), "chapelle" (chapel), "jardin" (garden). Pronunciation tips help: "château" becomes "shah-toh," emphasizing the long final vowel characteristic of Loire Valley French.

Wine tasting vocabulary transforms casual sips into cultural connections. "Dégustation" (tasting) initiates experiences, while descriptive terms paint sensory pictures: "fruité" (fruity), "boisé" (woody), "pétillant" (sparkling). Regional expressions add depth: "ça pinote" means "it's going well," referencing pinot noir grapes.

Restaurant interactions flourish through prepared phrases. "Une table pour deux, s'il vous plaît" (a table for two, please) begins dining adventures. "L'addition, s'il vous plaît" (the bill, please) concludes meals gracefully. Menu navigation improves through key terms: "entrée" (starter), "plat principal" (main course), "dessert" (dessert).

Market shopping reveals local character through language. "C'est combien?" (how much?) enables price inquiries, while "Je voudrais" (I would like) precedes selections. Numbers flow more naturally through practice: "quatre-vingt-dix" (90) becomes intuitive rather than mathematical.

Transportation terminology smooths daily movement. "Aller-retour" (round trip) and "billet" (ticket) facilitate train travel, while "prochaine arrêt" (next stop) aids bus navigation. "Où est...?" (where is...?) helps locate destinations, though regional pronunciation might soften final consonants.

Emergency phrases provide essential security. "Au secours!" (help!) and "J'ai besoin d'un médecin" (I need a doctor) prepare for urgent situations. Police understand "J'ai perdu..." (I've lost...) or "On m'a volé..." (I've been robbed...), though such needs rarely arise.

Cultural understanding enhances language effectiveness. Formal "vous" shows respect toward strangers and elders, while informal "tu" requires explicit invitation. "S'il vous plaît" and "merci beaucoup" demonstrate courtesy that Loire Valley residents deeply value.

Regional expressions color conversations distinctively. "Être en goguette" describes festive moments, while "avoir la goutte au nez" suggests wine appreciation. These phrases, when appropriately used, spark genuine smiles from locals who appreciate efforts to embrace regional character.

Pronunciation improves through pattern recognition. Loire Valley French tends toward softer consonants and longer vowels than Parisian French. Digital resources like Forvo provide native speaker recordings, while local radio stations offer immersive listening practice.

Success in Loire Valley communication stems from combining basic phrases with cultural awareness. Understanding context while maintaining humble learning attitudes creates meaningful interactions. Most importantly, each linguistic attempt builds connections, transforming simple transactions into opportunities for cultural exchange.

Between ancient words and modern expressions lies opportunity for genuine communication. Through thoughtful language use, travelers become participants rather than observers, their efforts to speak French enriching every Loire Valley experience while creating lasting connections with this remarkable region's inhabitants.

Printed in Dunstable, United Kingdom